DON'T GO
TO JAIL!

DON'T GO TO JAIL!

SAUL GOODMAN'S GUIDE TO KEEPING THE CUFFS OFF

Saul Goodman as Told to Steve Huff

THOMAS DUNNE BOOKS   ST. MARTIN'S PRESS   NEW YORK

THOMAS DUNNE BOOKS.

An imprint of St. Martin's Press.

DON'T GO TO JAIL! Copyright © 2016 by TM & © 2016 by Sony Pictures Television, Inc. All rights reserved. Printed in the United States of America. For information, address St. Martin's Press, 175 Fifth Avenue, New York, N.Y. 10010.

www.thomasdunnebooks.com

www.stmartins.com

Designed by Steven Seighman

Library of Congress Cataloging-in-Publication Data

Names: Goodman, Saul, (Fictitious character), author.
Title: Don't go to jail! : Saul Goodman's guide to keeping the cuffs off /
   Saul Goodman.
Description: First edition. | New York : Thomas Dunne Books, 2016.
Identifiers: LCCN 2015043622| ISBN 9781250078872 (hardcover) |
   ISBN 9781466891401 (e-book)
Subjects: LCSH: Better call Saul (Television program)—Miscellaneous. |
   Lawyers—Humor. | BISAC: HUMOR / Form / Parodies. |
   PERFORMING ARTS / Television / General.
Classification: LCC PN1992.77.B455 G68 2016 | DDC 791.45/72—dc23
LC record available at http://lccn.loc.gov/2015043622

Our books may be purchased in bulk for promotional, educational, or business use. Please contact your local bookstore or the Macmillan Corporate and Premium Sales Department at 1-800-221-7945, ext. 5442, or by e-mail at MacmillanSpecialMarkets@macmillan.com.

First Edition: April 2016

10 9 8 7 6 5 4 3 2 1

Contents

DON'T GO
TO JAIL!

Introduction

"Saul Goodman, at your service. Have a seat; let's talk about how I'll extract you from the fresh pickle you've nestled yourself into."

Imagine that the preceding statement was accompanied by a firm, warm handshake. An "old friend" strength grip with "reliable business acquaintance" brevity. That's what you'd get if you walked into the air-conditioned offices of Saul Goodman & Associates in Albuquerque, New Mexico, a refuge from the dry hellscape outside.

In this topsy-turvy economy of ours, I'm always open to new business. I figured I'd take a different lawyer tack and put something out there that tells prospective clients more about how I might approach the job of representing you, sprinkling in a few of my perspectives on life, the law, and everything.

Starting with: "privilege." It's a heavy word—got a lot of baggage on it these days. In the context of the attorney-client relationship, though, privilege is a wonderful thing. It means you get to tell me what's going on without having to worry if it's ugly or sounds bad or feels more rotten than that jack-o'-lantern your neighbors left out past New Year's. I'm here for immoral support, and that means breaking down your case and looking at all its unattractive parts so that we can be honest about what needs to be done. It's all between us, our little Cone of Silence.

This, what you're looking at right now? This is privileged. Unless you picked this book up at the library, it counts as the proverbial dollar in my pocket, and everything I tell you from here on out is just between us. Your secrets are safe with me under threat of disbarment—and as long as you're listening, I'm going to use this opportunity to give you a picture of why I do what I do and how this advice might be of use to you in the future.

Don't get me wrong; I'm damned sure not trying to make a lawyer out of you. There are too many creatures swimming, floating, and sinking in the attorney pond already. If anything, we could stand to fish out a few whose lack of legal talent could be better misused else-where.

I can't provide some kind of encyclopedic look at the legal system, either. Forget the lawyer pond—the legal system is a vast, endless ocean filled with sharks and krill and unrecycled bottles of Diet Coke. And as pretty as a tropical fish might be, most of what you're going to catch out there is your boring, run-of-the-mill tuna. Nobody wants to look too closely at those floppy things except other fishermen—or, in this case, other lawyers. What I *can* do is bottle up the most useful parts of that deep, expansive body of knowledge and offer you a few delicious drops of my legal cod liver oil. You know, for your health.

Were I a poet, I would pen this as a real guide—not just to surviving, but thriving, reviving, and moving on. I mean, if I wanted to get really Pollyanna about this grinding monster of a legal system that chews people into pieces and spits them into sunless cells every day of the week, I could say it's about renewal! Renewal of the righteous rule of law, each and every day! Renewal of the person! In some cases: yay, prison! Get renewed and ready for your life after correction via the healing power of twenty-three-hour lockdown in cellblock eight!

But you and I, we know things don't work that way.

That doesn't mean I'm ever going to advise anyone to

give up. In this quiver full of legal arrows on my back there isn't a single dud labeled, "Accept Defeat." Not my style. No one's looking for an attorney like that, anyway. A lot of people have walked through my office doors trapped inside some kind of glass box of empty desperation—I don't think a single one of them was looking for a guy who would say, "Yeah, this sucks, plead guilty, tee time's in thirty." Legal practices are chock-full of those types. We've all seen them: they work in big, shiny office buildings and have junior attorneys handling all the grunt work while they lean back in their ergonomic office chairs and rub magazine samples of Davidoff's Cool Water onto their wrists.

Oh, fine. In fairness, no working lawyer would do that anyway, as it would ensure disbarment faster than a buttered bullet can pierce a slice of toast. That's not to say they don't try.

Anyway, I've filled this treasure chest of a book with thoughts for your application and enjoyment; you're welcome. The law itself is a disorienting clown show of the random and the insanely, restrictively organized. If I'm being truthful—and I am, as you grant me a little reverse privilege here and will thus keep everything I say between us—I'm amazed the law works as well as it does sometimes. It can feel like the legal system is just one seemingly pointless new statute or one crazed Supreme Court ruling away from completely falling apart.

Look at some of the nutso laws that are still in place: in New Mexico, there's still a law that says "idiots" can't vote. It was created more than one hundred years ago when assholes used the word "idiot" to describe people who had some kind of learning disability, but it's still on the books. It's not enforced now, though, because imposing the modern definition of "idiot" would impede a majority of our beloved brethren from exercising their civic duty. In Massachusetts, there are still laws banning Quakers and witches. The state of Georgia has a law that criminalizes putting donkeys in bathtubs.

I'm not licensed in Georgia, but if you go there with the intent of lighting some candles and letting poor Eeyore enjoy a therapeutic soak, I'll track down someone good to represent you. We won't let anyone stop you from keeping your ass clean.

The law can be completely bonkers, but it still works. Attorneys are one of the big reasons why. We're up there scurrying along the battlements and manning cannons and you can fill in some more military images if you want, because I'm belaboring the point, which is: when you lawyer up, you have a kind of soldier on your side.

What you're reading doesn't detail legal strategies

and it also doesn't delve into just how much slow, tedious, eye-shriveling work can go into this trade. If you hate mind-numbing forms, thorny contracts, and endless blocks of text that contain umpteen semicolons and only one period, never even for a moment consider going into law.

If we're digging through discovery of the financial sort for one case, one day, we have to plow through countless pages of spreadsheet printouts trying to spot just one teeny-tiny set of specific numbers. We get all up in that haystack looking for a hay-colored needle. The next day, we could be reading police reports that manage to make a gruesome homicide sound dry and tedious. And we have to fill out forms and write letters galore pretty much every day. There was a kind of deliberate, serious TV show in the late 1970s about a law student, and it was titled *The Paper Chase* for a reason, because that's what we do. Sometimes I have nightmares I'm trapped in a Sisyphian document review session, endlessly combing through the same box over and over again until paper cuts have rendered my fingerprints unrecognizable, my locked-jaw molars ground down to the gums.

This is one guy's ad hoc look at how it works, from his own perspective. I'm okay if it pisses you off a little—not at me, necessarily, no, but at the way things work sometimes. And the way they don't. Sometimes the law doesn't quite serve everyone as it should. Too often, the law works against the regular guy. The working man. Average Joe Johnson and his garden ephemera store. Single-mom Suzy and her booming wedding photography business. It's set up to work to the state's advantage. People laugh about attorneys who put their faces on bus benches and make flashy commercials, call us ambulance chasers or whatever—but we aren't aiming at the country club set. Those people have white shoe firms on retainer, one quick phone call away. Small practices scrapping away are doing it for the folks who *work* in the country clubs. Who ride a bus or two to get to the daily grind. So that's where I put my face—right where those noble Americans can see it and rest their weary backs. Lawyers like me aren't superheroes, no, but we're doing a job plenty of other attorneys turn down in order to pursue the scent of that sweet, sweet corporate green. The system sucks and someone has to fight it on your behalf. I'm that guy.

And if you happen to catch sight of my advertisements while driving to your snazzy corner office in a hand-waxed Mercedes, hey—I won't turn you away, either. You might find that you like the more personal touch you receive from a single-counsel firm that has just the right pinch of razzmatazz.

PART I

How to Be
Your Own Attorney

⚖

Why You Shouldn't
Be Your Own Attorney

A real, battle-tested, State Bar of New Mexico–certified attorney is about to tell you it's a bad idea to attempt self-representation in a court of law. Most of the time. I know, I know—you were expecting an honorary law degree on this page, I'm sure. Don't put the book down quite yet. I'm here to inform you that, contrary to what your dear sweet Mama Bear has been telling you since she made you fess up to Mr. Hill about who touched the classroom's eye-wash station and accidentally flooded Little Billy's terrarium: sometimes you cannot handle your problems by yourself. I'm sorry. Sometimes the mud doesn't turn back into nice, dry dirt.

Trust me when I say that what you're reading here isn't meant to make a statement about any reader's smarts—you're reading this, so you're obviously intelligent and have impeccable taste—it's just about having faith in a certified attorney's ability to guide clients through the system. And smarts aren't the only thing that separates a lousy lawyer from the cream of the crop! More often than not, the best lawyer out there is a B+ student with the work ethic of an ox yoked to flaming plow. We want to do our jobs right (for reasonable fees and relevant expenses), and we've got a fire lit under our asses!

I'm sure you are an upstanding citizen with two-point-five kids packed in the back of your minivan, a fine American Kennel Club–registered breed of pooch sticking its head out the passenger window, washing the side mirrors with its suburban saliva. Or maybe you're a confirmed bachelorette with a nomadic streak, moon-lighting around the southwest selling hand-painted signs, a few buckets of acrylics, and some scraps of wood tucked away in your motorcycle's saddlebags. Either way: life is good, right? And for most, life will continue that way. Most people will never have to deal with anything more serious than a traffic ticket.

For that minor, piss-ant traffic ticket, you *may* be okay handling yourself in court. But the fact is, for just about everything else, you will probably need someone in your corner who knows what they're doing. A public defender, even. They get a bad rap, but I can tell you that most defense attorneys in the employ of a county or city office are just as passionate as private attorneys when it comes to helping defendants work their way through all the poisoned spike-filled traps hidden in the dark shadows of this treacherous jungle of a legal system. They just tend to have fewer windows in their sardine-can government offices.

Once you're in the system, you are a lost hiker, separated from your party in the Himalayan foothills. Think of us attorneys as your Sherpas. We are highly skilled mountaineers, and we've figured out when to swing our pickaxes into the ice to reach that next giant birch tree of dismissal or protective chasm of continuance. We know how to rescue you from the claws of the assistant DA and keep you from getting overwhelmed by altitude sickness. If you want to turn into Pro Se José and climb Everest alone, no helpful guide to point you in the right direction and carry your sleeping bag, I won't stop you! But I'd like to make sure you know what you're getting into, so here are some reasons to reconsider:

DON'T GO TO JAIL!

- **The even money on people defending themselves is they *will* screw it up.** Hell, you've probably even heard that dusty old line about actual trained attorneys representing themselves—that we'll never have a bigger fool for a client. The law is full of rules, subrules, clauses, and demands on plaintiffs and accusers. There are hard-and-fast requirements for submitting particular documents, which must be immaculately worded in keeping with, that's right, the law. Miss a court deadline for filing for an extension? Soon Oprah's shouting "YOU get a contempt citation! YOU get a bond revocation!" Think about it. You're facing, say, a DUI or a simple misdemeanor assault charge. Things are already stressful enough, don't you think? You don't want to spend all day studying up at the library computer terminals, wedged in between two public masturbators, just to realize when it's time to print that the government-funded copy machine is out of paper. There are folks who learned how the system works because we actually wanted to, and we could sure use your business. Not to mention the business of all those Johnny Jack-Offs who refuse to exercise their right to privacy in the comfort of their own homes.

- **Opponents will treat you exactly as they treat the most expensive legal eagles in the state.** No mercy, folks. Judges and prosecutors aren't your fairy godparents; they don't find their sole purpose protecting you and figuring out what will make you happy. They won't be like Great Aunt Ida at Christmas and applaud how cute you look in that holiday sweater, amidst all that *objecting* and *demanding*. No one serves juice and cookies in judges' chambers. Well, they may serve them to the judge. But lay legal warriors? Nope.

  To their credit, judges frequently question defendants who want to act as their own counsel. They'll try to figure out if you're sane, then tell you what I'm telling you, if they're the thoughtful type. The guys at the other table? They are *praying* to the old gods who eat souls and command sacrifice of little baby bunny rabbits that the judge does *not* talk you out of doing this. Then, if you go ahead, you will find they will be delighted to show you no mercy. No one will have any patience with the way you keep sliding to the bottom of the legal learning curve. It's brutal, and it is what men and women like me passed the bar to brave on your behalf.

- **Look at how long even the greenest attorneys take to get where you are.** This varies from lawyer to lawyer, but some of us spend a decade or more receiving our education, only to perform what amounts to apprentice work. The point being, this is hard work—which is why some in the legal community might feel even more antagonistic than usual if you come striding in proclaiming to represent yourself. You wouldn't walk up to a zookeeper and say, "Hey, let me feed that ferocious lion today. How hard could it be?" That zookeeper is going to be laughing a lot harder than you are, pal, as he shovels your chewed-up biceps into the hyenas' food trough. Attorneys can be prickly— sometimes the emphasis is on "prick"—about the difference between what it actually takes to do this job and what people might think it takes as they march in without preparation and try to do it.

  Would it help if I compared it to being a dentist? Sure, of *course* I can open an old toolbox right now and grab some vice grips. Absolutely, I could wipe 'em down, make sure they're reasonably clean, then stick them in my mouth and yank out this one molar that's been giving me fits. Then I could pack in some gauze or a wad of toilet paper and wait for the bleeding to stop, provided blinding pain hasn't laid me out already. I could do all that. But I could *also* go to Dr. Happy McPainFree on Novocaine Street, have him or her numb my screaming gums, then use what I hope are perfectly sterile instruments to take care of the problem. Still some pain, and it will cost me money, but it will get done right, and hopefully I won't bleed to death just because of a bad tooth. See, most people know it isn't wise to throw themselves on the mercy of the tooth fairy. In this case, the tooth fairy is a steel-eyed judge with a penchant for whack-a-mole and the gavel to prove it.

- **Acting as your own attorney will probably cost more money than hiring an attorney.** It will. I feel like I should repeat this about ten more times. Because acting as your own attorney almost definitely will cost you more money than just hiring counsel in the first place. The main reason? Chances are you will lose the case, be found guilty, and have to do some kind of time (or if you are super lucky, probation). Oh, and fines. The civil servants on the other side of that courtroom—if we're talking about criminal law—have salaries to fund, they have other budgets to make, and fellow prisoners in the county jail to feed cheeseburgers and grape juice. And those fines, especially if you've fumbled at the law like you're a pair of tenth-graders in the backseat of a Subaru, could be steeper than if you'd had a professional in court negotiate on your behalf. And civil court? Holy cats. Represent yourself civilly and you could end up on the hook for court costs and attorney fees on the other side. Those guys have the finest suits and biggest offices in the slickest buildings, and they will not hesitate to put you on the hook for everything if you are the losing party.

Let's pause, take a breath, and hope I've made my point before I go on. I admit that there will always be a few special souls who are convinced they can go it alone. And if you're one of them, I applaud your moxie. Because to face a court of law with your wits and whatever legal training you picked up from the Google school of law— and that one cousin who's been to jail so much he really *knows stuff, man*—takes courage.

So you're ready, you say. Stand at the courtroom doors. Take a deep breath. Kick open the gates to your salvation, and pray you've done some of the things I'll list below.

And remember, this is just a skeleton guide. I'm offering you the bare bones strategy of representing yourself in a court of law. It's up to you to put the skin on, by way of involved, intense, in-depth research on your own. (Don't even try to fake the guts and organs; it won't work and you don't have enough time to try.)

IF AT ALL POSSIBLE, LIVE INSIDE A COURTROOM

No, don't set up a tent and a Coleman stove and sing campfire songs with the bailiffs. What I mean is: head to your local courthouse and sit in on a few proceedings. Many courthouses have hearings open to spectators and believe me, there will be spectators. Journalists, cops with an interest in a particular case, families of the people involved, you name it. My favorites are the people who just like to hang out because it's interesting to them. Some of them are kind of weird, sure, and probably attend strangers' funerals, too. But if you were to set up camp in a courtroom, they'd be the ones to join along in campfire songs, not the bailiffs. Anyway, get in there and get a feeling for how things work. And forget what I said about campfires in the courtroom, that's the first thing they advise against in "Arson for Dummies."

FIGURE OUT THE BASICS

By basics, I mean rules and procedures. Every court has a set of them and they can be incredibly, ridiculously detailed. Get them from the court clerk and learn them like you're converting to a new religion and they comprise the holy book. If the Word of the Judge is that anyone born in the month of May must air guitar for two minutes to "Purple Haze" before addressing the court, then you'd better channel Hendrix and set that invisible Strat on fire. Judges won't have rules that whimsical, but you can see where I'm going with this.

Most remaining bookstores, the ones that haven't lost the fight against the Internet, will have shelves upon shelves packed with books chockfull of helpful information about the law. Buy those books. Keep reading this book, obviously, but also buy them. Dust off those number 2 pencils and grab every legal pad you can find—they're called *legal* pads for a reason!—and that will bring us to . . .

BREAK THE CASE INTO PARTS

Step one: you gotta pay close attention to the trees in order to understand the forest. I'm not referring to the massive quantities of paper consumed by even the smallest practices as we diligently pursue our clients' best interests—I'm encouraging you to examine the elements of the case you're embarking to defend. This is probably good news for you, because the job ahead can look like a big brown avalanche of crap, and it's your job to strap on the ol' flood pants, wade into that fetid pile, and parse each individual bowel movement. Maybe I'm not helping with that comparison. I'm just saying: take the case apart, piece by piece, and figure out how to prove each part. Real quick, here's a look at the usual elements of something civil, like negligence.

Let's say a retail business in a wintry city has a *duty* to customers to keep the sidewalk in front of the store clear of snow and ice. One hard winter, the manager feels a little shoulder strain while shoveling and looks around, figuring half-done is done enough. But wait! There's still ice on that walk! And along comes a young man in his prime, not wearing cleats or spikes or whatever, because he's not a soccer player and he's pretty used to trusting that businesses have their customers' safety in mind and are going to shovel their walks. *Whooosh!* This young man takes a header on the slick sidewalk, gets a concussion, or throws out his back. He gets hurt, this poor kid. How will he ever be able to cheer on his dear mother at her weekly pinochle tournament? All because the man in charge of the store, in a moment of weakness, *breached his duty* to his customers.

If the young man doesn't work out something with the store owner on the spot—some baseline fee just to keep the courts out of it—and he decides to sue, he has to prove that *but for* the icy sidewalk, he would never have cracked his skull or slipped a disc or wound up with whatever injury it was that he suffered. Also, he's got to prove that the defendant here, Mr. Rushy St. Business-man, could have easily predicted what was going to happen. In this case, I can guarantee for a fact the business owner knew the potential consequences. So those are the first parts: the who, what, when, where, why, and how.

The last piece of the puzzle is determining what the *damages* are. That ties everything together, as we add up the young man's medical bills and all his traumatic pain and suffering. Once we can put a number on that, we've tied the knot on this cherry stem of a negligence case.

LEARN RULES OF EVIDENCE

Evidence is everything, and there are rules for dealing with it. They can be pretty complicated, so turn into that obnoxious kid in class who raises her hand after every sentence her teacher says when it comes to asking questions about rules of evidence. You might be able to fumble some other details and survive, but without the admissible documents or whatever other evidence you've got to support your case? Might as well give the bailiff your jumpsuit measurements and bid farewell to your grandma—it's over the river and through the wood to the state penitentiary you go. You're screwed unless you get the evidence situation on lockdown.

I'm not going to sugar-coat this point: rules of evidence can be a bear. Not a cuddly Teddy Bear with button eyes—a ferocious hiker-eating grizzly type bear. Here's just one example of the way that bear can eat up precious brain-space: in the Federal Rules of Evidence, Rule 401 tells how to figure out whether evidence is actually relevant to the case or not. It says evidence is relevant if it "has any tendency to make a fact more or less probable than it would be without the evidence" and also "is of consequence in determining the action." Almost as simple as legal language ever gets. But—*then* there are paragraphs of notes below those points that go deeper and deeper into what makes a relevant piece of evidence and why. If your eyes aren't crossing by the end of paragraph two, it will be a minor miracle. If you don't want to walk into court and slop folders and boxes full of documents and transcripts in front of the judge only to have him or her rule it's all completely useless regarding your case, you will want to have a nodding acquaintance with those notes as well.

And that's just Rule 401. There are hundreds of Federal Rules of Evidence.

DEPORTMENT ISN'T ABOUT LEAVING THE COUNTRY

What's the first rule of topless beach volleyball? Don't be an asshole. This applies in court, too. Being polite and learning the right way to address the bench and the team on the other side can go a long way. I don't care if the judge looks like your estranged third cousin who ran off with your parents' only tractor—you call that woman "Your Honor." Also very important: dress well. The clothes make the lawyer! Or in this case, the citizen who is so bold that they think they don't need a lawyer. Get your hair done, throw some wax in your mustache, Polident your dentures to an ivory shine—clean up, but good.

It's vital that you play by these rules if you want to—at the very least—get through whatever you are doing in front of the court without looking like a complete schmuck.

So there it is—watch court happen, learn the rules, organize your arguments, get your evidence in order, be nice, and look snazzy. This whole law thing is a big ol' prickly patch of briars, and I could get all tangled up in need-to-know nuggets . . . but there just might be a different way out of this snare.

Buyer beware: this "different way" could be forced upon you, depending on the seriousness of the case. If you're up on a mass murder charge and figure, "Hey, I know the perfect defense for killing all those people and I'm the ideal person to present it," then it's a good bet the judge will appoint *standby counsel.*

Now be cool, don't worry! Standby counsel isn't there to bogart all the fun. No, this is an attorney whose job it is to guide you through this rocky terrain we've been talking about, and be on tap if—for whatever reason—you can't continue representing yourself. Like if you call your former buddy to the stand to ask him questions about why he got on your nerves so much during pub trivia that you had to tackle him in the bathroom and stuff urinal cakes in his mouth, but the sight of him makes you so upset that you become, shall we say, disruptive? In a case like that, the judge will ask your standby attorney to step in. They're your legal understudy, ready to play the role after you've danced yourself right off the front of the stage and broken both legs.

You know what I'm going to say, right? The best way to sum this up is "Hey, hey, don't!" The system sucks, yes, and it's often stacked heavily in favor of the court—but that's why guys like me are out here boiling water and building emergency lean-tos in the frozen wilderness every day, for clients like you.

What to Look for in an Attorney Who Isn't You

Ah, now we're going to have some fun. I'm going to make a few assumptions: that you are willing and hopefully able to hire legal counsel, and that you have the luxury of time. Time to research defense attorneys, weigh their strengths and weaknesses, time to decide whether they smell of bottom-shelf bourbon and discounted aftershave.

That's right, not all lawyers are created equal. After all, we're only people, just like you! We've all come to practice through different educational paths spanning a huge variety of learning institutions.

True, if an attorney has a degree from Columbia or Harvard Law, they've got a solid gold education behind them and were probably born with some high-wattage brainpower in the old *cabeza*. But that doesn't mean that every time they walk into a court of law they are going to completely smoke a competitor who pursued their legal education via correspondence or at an affordable night school. I've got to believe that the law's the law, no matter who you are. Sunbathing on a well-maintained Ivy League lawn with a heaping scoop of privilege in your parfait glass sure as hell counts for a lot in this world, but it doesn't automatically spell winner in the courtroom.

In fact, the night and correspondence school counselors are sometimes your best bets because they are, by far, the hungriest remoras hitching a ride on the great white shark that is legal practice.

Not to mention: education is one thing, cojones are another. Or, for the ladies—labia of steel? Think about it—do you want Mr. Cape Cod von Golfpants who can recite the history of rules of evidence backward while stirring the rocks in his Old Fashioned, or the ambitious gal who put everything on the line, working seven days a week and sleeping three hours a night to tame this wild beast that is the law, because she genuinely believed she could make a difference in her community? There's nothing more powerful than a true believer, my friend. Money can't buy sheer pluck.

Now that we've gotten that prejudice out of the way: let's break down what you want in any attorney, whether he studied at Harvard's Golden School of Legal Wizarding or at Little Donny's $5 Tattoo Parlor and Education Center.

LET'S GO TO THE ZOO!

In the legal zoo, there are two kinds of attorney. Behind the glass in the civil house we see the civil litigator. He or she is wearing high-end clothing, expensive hair products, and is parked in a gorgeous office building with a staff and sometimes several other lawyers of the same species. See those papers stacked neatly on their leather desk blotters as they relax for a moment with a game of Words With Friends or some choice pornography? Those documents are related to lawsuits.

It'd be easy for me to slam this as boring work, but it's not. Take, for example, the inmate at the Indian Creek Correctional Center in Chesapeake who filed a $5 million lawsuit against himself. It's true, ol' Robert claimed he violated his own civil rights in 1993 when he got drunk and subsequently arrested for grand larceny. He wanted to pay himself $5 million, but since he couldn't work and was a ward of the state, he politely asked that the state pay it on his behalf. Judge Rebecca didn't go for it, but I'm guessing she was entertained.

Civil law can bring in the big bucks for plaintiffs and for the attorneys, which is why we so often find them all gathered together in these offices like ants in an ant farm, just waiting for the next big cornflake to divide into pieces and carry off down their brightly lit tunnels, where they'll feed bigger chunks to the queens—senior partners—so everyone gets to grow fat together.

Now let's take a walk over to the big cats, the criminal defenders. These lions of legal acumen are sometimes alone, maybe working in smaller prides, and they live by different rules. They seek juicy red meat, not cornflakes or whatever else you feed ants.

How about I break down the differences even further?

- There's a different set of rules for the swarming civil attorneys on their lucrative diet of lawsuits than for the lean, hungry predators working criminal law. A historic case demonstrates the difference: People of the State of California v. Orenthal James Simpson. O.J.—who, say what you will, was pretty funny in the *Naked Gun* movies—was famously found not guilty of slashing his ex-wife Nicole Brown Simpson and young Ronald Goldman to death. His legal team demolished the state's case with rhetoric, psychology, and a little sleight of hand.

  But then the victims' families took O.J. to civil court, where due to the changes in rules of evidence, the Juice was squeezed dry. He was ordered to pay several million dollars in damages. He remained a free man (at the time) but he would have that debt over his head for the rest of his life.

  O.J. was done in once his case went civil because the burden of proof suddenly switched. That big bloodstained burden had been resting *entirely* on the overloaded shoulders of the state of California, those fine civil servants who had to pile up enough evidence to prove his feet filled those stylish Bruno Maglis the night of the murders. In civil court, burden of proof was on the plaintiffs—and as the defendant, Juice had a heavier burden to prove as well. Because in civil court, the plaintiff only has to convince a judge or jury that most of the evidence proves their claim. A criminal case has to be proved beyond a reasonable doubt, and we're talking something like 99 percent certainty there. Civil case? An easy 50 percent proof. It wasn't hard to get that in O.J.'s civil case, obviously.

- **Simplest difference between civil and criminal, which you could infer from Simpson's long, strange trip through the California courts: civil law is all about the money, honey.** Lose a civil case? No jail. Sure, that might change later if the loser of a given case is found in contempt for not obeying a court order, but let's not get bogged down in those kinds of things. The headline here is that even after a civil court found that O.J. did it, he still went home and slept in his own bed.

- **Let's say someone is beaten up by a domestic partner.** Serious, criminal stuff. Cops arrive, try to figure it out, separate everyone, and end up concluding the batterer needs to go to jail on an assault charge. A strange thing sometimes happens at this point: the victim will plead with the police to not arrest their partner. They'll even say they don't plan to press charges. Guess what? If the prosecutor gets a look at the case and all the evidence and decides a crime occurred, they'll press charges anyway. In criminal law, the victim doesn't have to cooperate. Different situation with civil cases.

Imagine waking from an appendectomy and feeling kind of achy and lumpy where your appendix used to be. You get an X-ray and lo and behold, some idiot was too busy scoping the hot nurse at his side and not your internal organs and he forgot where he put his surgical knife. Great negligence case there! But that scalpel will keep setting off metal detectors from here to Calcutta unless you find another more-focused doctor to get back in there and take it out—and your case will sit in limbo until you hire a civil attorney.

- **Anyone who has been arrested has (hopefully) heard the sweet siren song, "If you cannot afford an attorney, one will be provided for you."** The Sixth Amendment, baby! It says the state is obligated to give criminal defendants the best damned defense a few hundred bucks will provide. Civil court is a different matter, because the law seems to feel like the stakes are a little lower, somehow.

After all, a criminal court judge can slap you in jail, which takes just about everything from you. A civil judge can order you to pay money, allow or deny benefits like welfare, or medical disability. So, if a creditor gets tired of flooding you with notices and obnoxious phone calls and sues, you either hire a lawyer or go it alone, because the law considers the situation a little less life-or-death. Too often, as I've mentioned, that may end badly for you. Truth is, it might end badly for you in criminal court with the provided attorney, too, but hey, at least the odds are a little more in your favor!

- Ever see a commercial from a law firm about some kind of class-action suit? "Were you prescribed Drug X and have you suffered the following side effects?" A list of stuff like dizziness, seizures, and, I don't know, suddenly finding yourself *really* into Swedish rap music from 1996 may follow. Many such commercials will contain a claim that the firm won't get paid unless you do. That's true, but if a criminal defender ever says he or she won't get paid unless they win your case, they're wrong. In civil law, a firm can work a case on the contingency they'll win. Obviously, they rarely do this unless it is a backboard-shattering slam dunk of a case. Criminal defense attorneys can't do that, it's against the law.

- **Another difference? Civil attorneys can work any side of a case.** In a case of negligence—like that theoretical surgical scalpel my theoretical Mc-Dreamy left parked somewhere near your small intestine—both sides will end up with civil attorneys working from the same sets of rules. Criminal defense attorneys never work for anyone but the man or woman up on the dock for some alleged crime.

To put a maraschino on top of this whipped-cream-coated sundae of law talk: the O. J. case proved the difference between civil and criminal burdens of proof. Here's why: in a criminal case, a defendant's counsel is a little more empowered. We can't let our clients incriminate themselves, and this can limit what the prosecution is able to present in court. In civil law, each side gets an equal bite out of the discovery apple, an equal opportunity to come away chewing on one damning half of a worm.

Now that I've whet your appetite for some differences in civil and criminal law—and trust me, buddy, this has just been the highlights—it's time for the nitty-gritty: how the heck do I pick a lawyer?

I've worked civil and criminal cases, but tend to park my Cadillac in the criminal lot more often than not. Most attorneys try a bit of both sides before settling on one. In criminal defense, my job has been to convert illegal drug addiction into legit drug prescription. To demonstrate in front of carefully selected juries of matronly, empty-nester housewives how shark-eyed assassins were once boys who never had a proper mother's love.

But I've known civil attorneys and had a taste of the practice, so what I'll do now is give you some tips for picking a legal representative from either type of practice.

GOOD VS. BAD

What does "bad" mean in this situation, really? What does "good" mean? It's all subjective, relative, and another "-ive" word of your choosing (maybe not "chive" or "contraceptive"). Just like a "no trans fat" label on a bag of chips—it depends on what you're going for.

I can tell you this, though it gives me some pain to do so: flashy, well-produced ads do not *always* a good lawyer make (present company excluded). They just mean someone used a big hunk of the budget to rent billboard space and maybe hire a video crew to help them get facetime in front of you, their future client.

They do other clever things as well! Online, for example—doctors, lawyers, dog-grooming places, they all get reviewed on the Internet. Hell, there are sites where college kids discuss whether their professors were cool that one time the student accidentally called them "Mom," or the day a baggie of weed slipped from the kid's backpack.

It's convenient to believe that a slick-looking ad campaign or a bunch of glowing online reviews add up to a shining star pointing toward your legal savior. Not so. The reviews, like the ads, can simply be bought. There are folks who will pay $5 for someone to give their book about artistic nose hair snipping a rave review, and plenty who will take that five-spot and do it. So you better believe there are some in the legal community who hire summer interns solely to bump the firm's three-point-five star average to a solid four. Instead of starting your attorney search with the yellow pages—that plastic-wrapped book of ads and colored paper slowly decomposing on your front porch, for you kids reading this—ask for referrals from people who've been in your stinky shoes.

Example: from the criminal end of things—you were at the bar and tied on a few. Got in the car to head home and next thing you know, there's a Kmart blue light special going on in your rearview. Only the officer who approaches the driver's side isn't offering you great deals on impact sockets, he or she is ready to breathalyze you into a holding cell. Now you've got a DUI. If we assume for the sake of the story that this was a relapse, it might be a time to get thyself to a meeting and ask your fellow anonymous alcoholics if they know of any attorneys who are good at handling these sorts of things.

This approach to getting a lead on a good lawyer is preferable to flipping a phone book open to the attorneys page, shutting your eyes, and dropping your finger on an ad. The yellow pages won't make for a good Ouija board. Ask your family, ask your friends—they're good for more than just last-minute rides to the airport.

Similarly, there are basic rules for selecting a civil attorney, even down to the group research level. Say a loved one tragically passed and it looks like hazardous working conditions contributed to their death—asbestos, toxic chemicals, that nasty stuff. In that instance, rather than playing Russian roulette with your local lawyer options, go sit down with a group of survivors. This isn't an uncommon thing now. If you know the name of an attorney who interests you from seeing some brilliant ad campaign, look him up in old newspapers, do a little detective work online. Have they won similar cases? Did they get huge honking loads of *dinero* out of the evil fat cats they recently sued? Civil counsels' legal records are public record, you just need to track them down.

It's easy for firms to buy up ad time, but it's important to pay attention to what they've done, not just what they say they'll do.

I'm not 100 percent against using whatever means necessary to get to the right man or woman for your legal needs. If you like, you can check out bar-approved lawyer referral services, but those might not give you a complete picture of your future legal savior, either.

Remember, the attorney works for you. Fellow doctors of jurisprudence will probably be pissed at me for pointing this out, but it's perfectly okay for a potential client to interview an attorney to see if the chemistry is right. I'm confident in my abilities to perform—you can speed-date as many lawyers as you like; I have a feeling I'm going to be the guy you're going home with. After a few dates, go with your gut and make it official with the right suitor for your legal suit.

That is: we've gotten this far and you've found a counselor who hits your sweet spot. Maybe you like what you've seen attached to their name in the papers. Maybe you like the Maltese Falcon statue on their desk. Maybe you just like the strawberry candies they put out in their reception area. If they say they're open to the thrilling adventure that is every new client, you've reached a crossing.

This is your opportunity to decide whether you want to hire this person. And all that stuff about what to look for won't amount to a hill of beans if you sit down, stare that counselor in the eye, and think, "No way do I want this asshole to have my finances, my criminal record, or God forbid my life in his hands." But if you like it (it being your future lawyer), put a proverbial ring on it. Pull the trigger, dive in. Ride off into the Just Lawyered sunset, or at least toward the long honeymoon of your case procedure.

WHAT TO LOOK FOR WHEN YOU INTERVIEW A PROSPECTIVE ATTORNEY

Some of this might seem like common sense, yes. But a little tough love, if I may: sometimes people end up needing a lawyer because what they really needed in the first place was some common sense. Everyone has lapses in judgment from time to time—vision cloudy, idle hands becoming the devil's plaything and what have you. Nothing to be ashamed of, but we're going to measure twice and cut once to make sure you're crystal clear about what you're looking for in your would-be counsel.

Let's get to it, then.

Say you get an appointment with an attorney. Casual

coffee meet and greet, in-office confab, hang-gliding trip across one of the great southwestern deserts— whatever sweeps your sand. This first interaction is vital. Go in with this mercifully short checklist of things to look for.

I call what follows "The Other Big Cs."

- **Chemistry.** We all know speed-dating works like this: you've got three-to-five minutes to decide if there's some magic spark that will eventually lead to some binding and grinding between you and that equally nervous person nursing a mai tai on the other side of that tiny round table, right? You have to judge their teeth, their hair, eye contact, shoulder-width, pore-size—all in noth- ing flat.

    Good news! You've got way more time than that when you first encounter prospective legal counsel. Personality in this case is paramount. It doesn't matter how well-recommended that attorney is, doesn't matter how much the cameras love them when they're on the courthouse steps— if anything about that attorney makes you feel uneasy, sleazy—hell, even sleepy—they aren't the counselor for you. This is an instance when gut instincts are your best friend, because the hard truth is if you and this vessel of legal wisdom just don't harmonize, the entire case will go horribly out of tune. You two will be like Simon and Cher, Sonny and Garfunkel. It won't work.

- **Communication.** To put it bluntly, we lawyers can suck at communicating with clients efficiently. I wish it wasn't true, but it is. So this is what you do on your low-speed date with prospective Counselor X: clarify the best way to communicate and what sort of turnaround to expect. Like, if you e-mail X's paralegal to see if you need to be there for the next court date, can you expect a reply sometime before the actual court date? You don't want to be hanging out by the pool halfway through a second pitcher of margaritas only to get a panicked call asking why the hell you aren't in court.

Where we lack in communication, we make up in performance. You'd be surprised at how often attorneys have performing-arts backgrounds—music, theater, musical theater, it varies. A truly charming and engaging counselor tethered to a hang glider could still drop the ball when it comes to simply clarifying whether you need to show up for a court date or not, but may dazzle every judge this side of Justice Street.

And hey, it's understandable that lawyers occasionally have issues keeping clients informed. Say it's a lone wolf practice, only a secretary and the attorney. Just to break even and pay off their loans, that lawyer has to take on as many cases as he or she can reasonably manage. Everyone's idea of what the word "reasonably" means is a little different. So it's easy to get overwhelmed. The problem with that is judges (who were often lawyers themselves and can be filled with self-loathing regarding their time in the trenches) have very little mercy on attorneys who forget shit or misspeak. Already you can see how easy it is for even a gifted attorney to become overwhelmed.

Putting your prospective attorney on the spot in the first meeting about methods and speed of communication will at least make it clear to counsel that you expect to stay informed in a timely manner. Any attorney comfortable with this setup is a good bet for you.

- **Compliance.** I'm not sure "compliance" is the best word for this point, but it makes the whole "Other Big Cs" scheme work out great, so screw it, I'm going with it. It does pretty much fit this important point: you've got to feel that the attorney you're scoping out is flexible and open-minded enough to really work with you. They have to go with your wishes, within reason. That is, if your wishes are really stupid and self-defeating, it's also an attorney's obligation to tell you so and try to steer you in a better direction. Example: if a client walks in and says, "I wanna go to court in my unitard hot dog costume because I just got baptized at the Church of the Non-Apostolic Wiener God," it's an attorney's job to say, "Eh, not so sure about that."

That's where you come in—be steerable. Leave the unitard at home. Compliance is a two-way street, and an attorney can only do so much good for a stubborn client. To truly be *muy simpático*, clients need to come into a relationship with a new attorney like baby birds, ready to slurp up all the legal goodness we're trying to regurgitate into their hungry mouths.

I'm well aware that some prospective clients need a road map, a list of things to do. I'll close out this part of our chat with something you can write down or bookmark. Go ahead, take it with you to all your future meetings, and ask the following questions before you put your legal life in someone else's hands:

SAUL GOODMAN'S HANDY LIST OF QUESTIONS TO ASK ANY ATTORNEY

1. **Have you done this before?** By "this," I mean the kind of case that has you in the hot seat. If they haven't actually been, you know, practicing the law, things are going to get a little awkward, and you may find that you walked into the wrong office suite. It's odd that no one mentioned anything before you sat down. But assuming you are in the right place: ask questions specific to your case. Every attorney has to learn their craft, but you don't want to be anyone's first time. Just invite a few exotic dancers to your nephew's bar mitzvah to discover how quickly and messily that can end.

2. **How are you going to do this?** Not with magic law beans. There are some moving parts to this one—what are the possible resolutions? Is there another way to go—that is, is this something that requires a lawyer? What approach will you take? Strategies in civil or criminal law can be as different as lawyers themselves. Some attorneys will be bulls. Some will be bulls in china shops. Others will be shaved sloths wearing expensive watches. Avoid the latter.

3. **How broke will I be?** Attorneys don't want you homeless or bankrupt—as that might send you to a different

lawyer altogether—but everyone wants to get paid. You have a right to see rates and to know when you will get the bill. Also, don't hesitate to ask for an estimate of what the final tally might be, once expenses and other fees are taken into account.

That's a good start, but we're not done yet. Just for fun, let's explore what happened to a few other folks who decided to go pro se. All smart guys, so what could go wrong?

Sir Walter Raleigh

Raleigh was a Renaissance man—he actually lived during the Renaissance. He was a poet, a lawyer, a colorful wild man about town, a noble at court . . . and he allegedly committed one of the finest moments of ass-kissing on record when, legend has it, he covered a puddle with one of his expensive cloaks so Queen Elizabeth could cross without getting her dainty feet wet. And even if Raleigh didn't really ruin a perfectly good cloak for points in the Queen's court, those who knew him could believe he did it.

He led a long and productive life, but in spite of his masterful ability to suck up to people in power he still ended up a prisoner in the Tower of London. Queen Elizabeth had died and King James wasn't about to be impressed by lesser nobles dropping cloaks over puddles on his behalf.

Sir Walter went up against a tribunal that accused him of plotting to bring down the King. He presented his own defense like a true master.

The case against him was pure olde bull shite and he knew it. Naming Lord Cobham, an accuser who'd written an affidavit against him then recanted, Raleigh said to the jury, "Consider, you Gentlemen of the Jury, there is no cause so doubtful which the King's Counsel cannot make good against the law. Consider my disability, and their ability: they prove nothing against me, only they bring the accusation of my Lord Cobham, which he hath lamented and repented as heartily, as if it had been for an horrible murder: for he knew that all this sorrow which should come to me, is by his means. Presumptions must proceed from precedent or subsequent facts."

"It's all hearsay and you know it," was Raleigh's point, and he wasn't just right, he was beautifully right. It might have been a peak moment for anyone defending anything in a court of law. But he was convicted and sentenced to death anyway, because it was a time in Merrye Olde Englande when the people in charge really enjoyed their regular days out chopping off the heads of the guilty, the just, and sometimes the guys the King thought looked at him funny that one time.

Only a last-minute reprieve from the King kept Sir Walter's head on his shoulders. Then, the royal decision-makers let him cool his heels in the Tower of London for the next thirteen years.

And though he was released and even went to South America searching for El Dorado, the legendary city of gold, Sir Walter Raleigh still ended up with his head on the chopping block two years after his sentence had ended.

So you can represent yourself with Shakespeare-level eloquence like Sir Walter Raleigh and still end up in the Tower, or worse. Also, poor guy never came anywhere near that City of Gold.

Representative James Traficant

Late congressman Jim Traficant was a pretty good example of a pro se defendant who had spectacular success. Look, a role model of sorts for you to hang your hat on! Maybe all my fuss about the dangers of self-representation was unfounded . . .

The honorable gentleman from Ohio was a humble county sheriff in the mid-1980s when he found himself facing charges of bribery and racketeering. He decided he was his own best defender and damned if he wasn't right! Jim Traficant had gone up against a case that fell under the Racketeer Influenced and Corrupt Organizations Act—RICO to folks who don't have all day—and he won. *No one* ever wins against RICO.

It gets better. Sheriff Traficant realized he'd developed serious name recognition in his district and he doubled-down: he wanted to be Congressman Traficant. He ran for the seat and won. Hell, he kept winning, returning to D.C. for eight more terms.

Then in the early 2000s, Traficant found himself in court again. Once again he was hit with his old nemesis, racketeering. Not to mention bribery and tax evasion.

Traficant figured he was still fighting the fight he'd won in the 1980s. Seeing no reason to reinvent the wheel, he defended himself—but it didn't go very well. It's tricky to say what a lawyer might have been able to achieve in his stead, but on his lonesome the congressman was convicted on ten felony counts and sentenced to federal prison. So, maybe he shouldn't be your historic North Star, either. Rats.

Give it to Jim, though—he wasn't about to let prison get in his way. He ran for his seat again while behind bars and still managed to snag 15 percent of the vote. He passed away five years after he was released from prison. I hope that even though he's gone, the possibility someone can beat RICO still lives on.

Ted Bundy

Time to get a little dark for a minute and talk about serial killers. Well, one serial killer. Teddy-boy, Theodore Robert Bundy, the clean-cut, affable face of butchering bright young college girls in the 1970s.

Ted was a shark in human disguise, complete with the classic dead fish gaze if the camera caught him at the wrong moment. On the surface he was a buttoned-down, conservative dude—a law student and wannabe politician. He even had a great courtroom voice: low, no identifiable accent, smooth as silk.

Ted's killing spree stretched from Washington State down to Florida, and he only grew more and more uncontrolled as he went. Weird thing about maniacs like Bundy—sometimes it seems like they can really control things enough to keep their awful hobby a secret until, well, they just can't anymore. That's what happened with Ted, he unraveled as he went south. Finally, one day, they had him in a Colorado jail, charged with murder.

It looked like old Ted, already convicted of kidnapping in Utah, was done. Just like that fad diet "You Are What You Eat"—Teddy looked like he was dead meat.

But he wasn't. Ted decided to put his legal education to work and told the judge in Colorado that he would act as his own attorney. At this point he was actually ahead of many pro se defendants—he had a little bit of solid legal education under his belt.

But he wasn't just trying to refine his courtroom skills, because serial killers aren't known for being straightforward like that. As his own counsel, this serial killer didn't have to wear cuffs or leg shackles (don't get any ideas—if you're ever in Young Master Bundy's position, that's not a thing in every court). One day, he used a research trip to a law library to escape.

He was recaptured pretty quickly and continued representing himself. Here's the crazier part: *the case was going Ted's way.* He had a legal adviser, but Ted was actually pretty sharp in the courtroom. He was knocking down weak evidence and motions from the prosecution right and left.

Psychopaths, though—they've always got to go down the psycho path. Ted went on a diet, managed to saw a small hole in the ceiling of his cell that he could get through with his thinned-down form, and escaped again.

This time he stayed gone for a little while. He zigged and zagged and ended up in Florida, calling himself Chris Hagen. Eventually, Ted lost what control he had and started killing again. But of course it wasn't any of the several murders and assaults he committed in the Sunshine State that tripped him up—it was that he was driving a stolen car.

As I like to warn people, it's always the little details that bite you in the ass.

Florida put Bundy on trial for murder, and it was a big show. Broadcast on TV, press from all over. And Ted had not just one, but *five* court-appointed lawyers at his disposal. So of course he chose once again to act in his own defense.

Ted and his advisers hammered out a plea deal with the prosecution. A plea deal in Florida, a state that's always had a real affection for putting folks in Old Sparky. He'd have to cop to the murders he'd committed, and for that he'd get seventy-five years. Seventy-five years in prison is no picnic, but he'd be alive.

He couldn't handle the fact he'd have to admit he'd savagely murdered innocent young women, though, so he went to trial.

This was Ted's first Florida trial, and he lost. But you know, he did make an impression on the judge, who said, "You'd have made a good lawyer. I would have loved to have you practice in front of me, but you went the wrong way, partner."

Ted kept going the wrong way. He defended himself in his next trial, too. Of course he lost, but let's give him credit for one clever legal move: he managed to marry his girlfriend while questioning her in open court, using a little known Florida statute that says if someone declares they are married in front of a judge, well, they are.

Bundy was executed in the late 1980s.

I have to give him credit—the guy took to the law like chloroform takes to a rag, and he pulled off a legit wedding ceremony quicker than I can Google "hubristophilia."

Larry Flynt, Porn Baron

After talking about something as heavy-duty as Ted Bundy's courtroom antics, I should probably lighten things up. I admit: there are some fascinating, if not necessarily fun stories of pro se litigants out there—people who went up against the system without much in the way of legal equipment and nailed it, knocked it out of the damn park. Especially in some civil court cases.

Larry Flynt comes to mind. The wheelchair-bound publisher of *Hustler* (also known as the glossy-paged erotica most likely to be found in that special spot under a growing boy's mattress), represented himself in court on a few occasions. He even tried to defend himself in front of the Supreme Court, but the highest court in the land wasn't having any of the porn king's crap. They appointed an attorney to address the court on Flynt's behalf. Flynt was so angry about that he acted up in court, yelling, "Fuck this court! You denied me the counsel of my choice." He said the justices were "eight assholes and a token [very impolite word that starts with a "c" and was directed at Justice Sandra Day O'Connor]." Larry Flynt: gifted pornographer, truly gifted demonstrator of contempt for the court.

Robert Kearns, Inventor

As bountiful as the tales of a filthy-mouthed porn king may be (and they be aplenty), inventor Robert Kearns takes the pro se story cake. Who the hell was he, you ask? Lean in, enjoy . . .

If you're driving along and it starts drizzling, your windshield gets hard to see through. If you run wipers full tilt, they do the job too well, right? They squeak until your teeth grind. One night, Robert Kearns was driving and it occurred to him that windshield wipers needed some kind of middle gear. He went home and invented the intermittent wiper you're probably still using on your vehicle today.

Kearns knew he was onto something and brought what he'd made to some big automakers. Nobody bit at the time, but in a few years, the same car companies had somehow magically added their own intermittent settings to their products' wipers. Go figure!

Kearns patented his invention in 1964. In the late 1970s, he realized he needed to bring suit against Ford Motors for infringing on his patent—they were using his invention and he wasn't seeing a profit! Guess what? Kearns won his suit. He won big, in fact—10 million bucks. But it wasn't easy. Kearns's case against Ford was his life. His fight with the big monolith that old Hank built went on through the 1980s. He had a nervous breakdown; his marriage broke apart. Eventually, he actually wore the company down. They got tired and offered him millions in compensation.

But he turned it down, and fought some more. It finally took a federal jury to put the kibosh on the guy's fight with Ford—the federal jury declared Kearns should get the $10 million. He then decided it was time for Chrysler to feel his wrath.

He faced Chrysler with a crew of lawyers, and they managed to persuade another federal jury that this genius's patent had been infringed. The case turned to the damages phase and that was when Kearns told his attorneys to get lost and took over himself.

Once again, he was like a pro se savant—he convinced the jury to award him $20 million in damages. Chrysler wisely appealed the case to the Supreme Court, but the highest court in the land didn't really satisfy anyone: the justices said Kearns should get his damages, but Chrysler couldn't be prevented from using intermittent wipers.

The Amazing Mr. Kearns wasn't done, believe it or not. He decided it was time to take on GM, as well as automakers from Europe to Japan.

That was when Kearns finally discovered his limits. He'd kicked plenty of ass, relentlessly so, but the amount of work was too much for one guy. Courts mostly dismissed his cases after that. In some ways, his mission— and this guy was on a mission—had finally overwhelmed him. I gotta hand it to him; for the right to be recognized as the dude who invented a middle wiper setting, he really maxed out the phrase "going the distance." Well done, Kearnsy. Well done.

And for all the tap dancing I'm doing to celebrate my line of work and encourage you not to go *mano y* gavel with the courts by yourself, I have to admit that it's still great that we all live in a land built to let us go it alone if we have to. Just remember the example of Robert Kearns. I admit, he had advantages: he was a brilliant guy, had a great education, even had experience working in military intelligence—but you don't need to have any of these things if you understand that handling your own case requires one thing above all: hours upon hours of bona fide home-grown elbow grease.

I won't say you'll win your case if you put that kind of sweat equity into it, but it will damn sure help.

What's Next?

Still with me?

We've taken a good, hard look at different sides of the question, "Should I be my own attorney?" Hopefully by now you're ready to call your own personal Saul.

Next, we'll tackle some common situations that can require counsel. If the next part of our extended little chat—aren't you glad I waived my usual fees for this?—does what I intend, it will ease the road through the legal system not only for you, but for your attorney, too.

I'll get into the stuff us lawyers wish our love-'em-but-they're-crazy clients would keep in mind before they speed-dial their weed dealers from the Dairy Queen parking lot, walk out of Kmart with a DVD player that "fell off the shelf," or tell Mr. Officer what to suck—I feel a migraine coming on just thinking about it. I'll also tell you what you can do to dodge the shit flying off the fan after you've ignored these soon-to-be-mentioned things to keep in mind before the shit hits the fan. Your dodging could mercifully spare me a stress-induced aneurism.

Life's too short to spend all your time under the state's flickering fluorescents, so the following is my gift to you, illustrating basic techniques and ways to look at certain situations, and how to—hopefully—safely get out of them.

If they work for you, feel free to recommend me to your friends, your family, your gastroenterologists. Like I said—word of mouth is worth a hundred billboards.

PART II

When You Need an Attorney

⚖

Warrants Schmarrants

Here's a potentially blood-pressure disrupting experience that hundreds, maybe thousands of our fellow citizens across America have every day. (Yes, I'm talking to
you. The Justice Department says you have a one in ten
chance of the following happening to you this year.)
You're out for a little Sunday drive, heading to the ice
cream shop or grabbing a bite at the Taco Cabeza, doing those things enthusiastic citizens do on Sundays,
when—*BLURRP*—is that an angry duck behind you?
Nope, it's a police cruiser's loudspeaker. Your rearview
is suddenly infested with the blue lights of your hardworking fellow Americans who just want to take a

glance at your license and registration. They could be searching for a terrorist, they could have received a tip that a nearby Pottery Barn was just burglarized by someone wearing a green hat just like yours, they could even just be checking to make sure little Benny's or precious June's car seat has been properly installed. All perfectly normal stuff, "reasonable suspicion" and all that. In their words, a "routine traffic stop."

The officer takes your license, strolls back to their Crown Vic to call it in. You're okay there in your vehicle—you know you weren't speeding, all your lights function, everything is gravy. Nothing to worry about.

Then *BAM*, next thing you know there's a grim voice over your left shoulder ordering you to "step out of the vehicle and keep your hands where I can see them," little Benny screaming in terror as Officer Friendly turns into Officer Unsympathetic. Your life has gone to hell in a hot second all because of one tiny little bench warrant.

A bench warrant is like an appendix—you could go most of your life not realizing yours was a ticking time bomb out to get you, until some kinda bad luck or imbalance or karma or wrath of whatever Higher Power you have comes along and suddenly it's a huge pain in your side. Bench warrants are the bane of people who are either forgetful, avoidant, or just plain lazy.

Here's how they're different from plain old everyday arrest warrants: an arrest warrant is a statement of probable cause. Officer Frick or Frack gives a formal statement to a judge that lays out all the reasons they believe someone committed a criminal act. Provided that the judge thinks the warrant is better than the unforgiving one-ply tissue they use in the courthouse restrooms, he or she will sign it. An arrest warrant is a little jolt of triple espresso in a cop's shitty vending machine coffee—they often run right out to make an arrest.

Bench warrants are issued by judges when the rules of the court are violated. Rules like showing up when you have a court date. Say it was a pretty day, and maybe you detoured through that nice little city park to better enjoy nature during your trip to the courthouse. Say you stopped by the pond there to enjoy the breeze and the sun. A friendly duck waddles up to you. Ducks with their crazy walks, right? You're just finishing your turkey sandwich, you can spare some of the crust, so you start tossing it to the ducks. Soon, you're surrounded by these ducks and fellow good folks enjoying the sunny park and what a day, right? Best ever.

While you are having that best day ever, there was a courtroom convened a quarter mile away ready to play "This is Your Life." Only, you didn't show up. In the eyes of the judge, you aren't interested in mending fences with the law. *BOOM*. Instant bench warrant, because not obeying an order to show up is contempt of court. And it doesn't even matter if you missed because of a flat tire or your niece's bat mitzvah or because your poor old grandma had an emergency gastrointestinal procedure—in the law's opinion, "No excuses!"

Unpaid child support can bring either an arrest or a bench warrant, depending on the state or the judge's mood. Not showing up for traffic tickets that require a court visit can definitely result in a bench warrant. Bench warrants are surprisingly easy to get, and a lot of otherwise good, law-abiding people have one out for them.

Thing about bench warrants is this—in many places, they just aren't a big priority to the police. They're likely addressed on occasion, when a few cops are free to do service duty. Or in a database to be accessed by the police dispatcher if your license number's called in during a minor traffic stop. Hell, if you're lucky, maybe someone got proactive and sent you notice by certified mail that there's one out for you—but you can't put a decent wager on that last scenario.

Without wasting time flipping through every possible reason a bench warrant could be looming in a computer system right now, ready to screw you, I'm going to dole out a few free tips on handling the lurking bench warrant menace.

WHEN YOU NEED AN ATTORNEY

What follows are guidelines on how to see if there's one out for you, what you can do if there is, and what to do if you end up riding out your sunny American Sunday afternoon in a holding cell that smells like it's been sprayed down by a skunk with a gland deficiency.

HELLO, IS IT ME YOU'RE LOOKING FOR?

This will seem kind of tricky—and if you have the cash available to hire a lawyer to do it for you, you should—but if you have a sneaking suspicion there might be a lonely little warrant sitting on a quiet bench just inside a judge's chambers in your town, or in a city where you've lived in the past, you may be able to get ahead of it. Or slightly less behind it, because some might say you were behind when you didn't do whatever it was that led the judge to sign the warrant in the first place.

This involves a little detective work. Modern detective work, not old-timey gumshoe stuff. First, go to your favorite Internet search engine and plug in the words "bench warrants" and your state of choice. Search results will throw a lot of attorney pages and ads for pay-to-search sites at you, but also websites like the Maricopa County, Arizona sheriff's page listing outstanding warrants with names and current (or more likely, former) addresses.

If that doesn't yield the intended results, it's time to

pick up the phone and get ready to make a new friend. If you're feeling a little paranoid, maybe don't use your own phone. There are plenty of solitary pay phones along Route 66 just begging for you to drop a dime in them without the worry of you accidentally dropping a dime on yourself.

- **Call the number of the sheriff's department for the county where you suspect the bench warrant waits and ask if they want to arrest you.** Just kidding! But it *is* usually sheriff's deputies who are charged with serving warrants and as with Maricopa County, they'll have a list—it's just not always on a helpful public site. Tell them you're asking for a friend of a friend.

- **Going to the people whose full-time gig is knocking on doors and dragging folks to jail is intimidating.** I understand! I've had undainty dalliances with several, deal with 'em daily, part of the job. If sheriff's departments are confusing or unnerving, here's a different civil servant worth approaching: the city or county clerk of courts. There's some comfort in talking to a "clerk" on the phone instead of a deputy. A clerk of courts is likely to have the information you need. In larger cities they'll sometimes have their own websites with searchable databases. Either way, they'll probably know if there is a warrant and what you need to do to make it go away.

- **If simple measures like getting in touch with the sheriff or the clerk of courts are dead ends, you better call a lawyer.** It's like I've been telling people since I passed the bar: we're insurance. Live in the shadow of Mount St. Helens? The bank holding your mortgage wants you to have volcano insurance, just in case old girl smells the Folgers and decides it's time to wake up again. Even if there's a chance nothing bad will ever happen, it's smart to be prepared. Imagining the worst can be scary! We lawyers are here to help you understand what's going on and guide you through taking care of it. A lawyer knows how to dig up the warrant and what to do about it.

THERE'S A BENCH WARRANT. OOPS.

Let's say you now know that bench warrant is lurking in the shadows and it's just a matter of time before it bites you on the ass. Now what?

If on your own you were able to pull up the details of your bench warrant—before you were arrested or had to hire a lawyer—and you're not too tense about the situation yet, handling the problem may be, believe it or not, as simple as contacting the court that issued it and saying, "Hey, help me get back on the right side of the law!"

As always, the response will vary, but if positive vibes are aplenty and everyone in those court chambers has eaten a balanced breakfast with a heaping side of goodwill toward their fellow man, they may be pretty helpful and tell you exactly what to do. They'll be serious and emphasize the importance of showing up and never admit bench warrants are the most passive-aggressive court document and you'll just have to take it. Then they may work with you!

Since we're talking bench here, as I've said already, there's a good chance it's for something minor like a traffic ticket. This can be your chance to not make a merely bad situation into an actual shitstorm. If you contact the issuing court and they say, "No problem, Mr. Good American Citizen, let's set up another court date!" That's actually great!

Just show up. Don't take a pleasant walk in the park to feed the ducks. Show up. I can't emphasize that enough. Because if a judge has already issued one bench warrant for a failure to appear, they will be more than happy to issue a second one, and this time it'll be even more likely to crack your bank account open like a lobster claw. Before they can slurp out all your juicy, hard-earned savings, turn to an attorney. Someone whose soothing voice breaks the bad news, then lays out your next steps and runs interference for you along the way.

OH, SHIT, I'M IN JAIL

Imagine that now we're back in that hypothetical holding cell with our unhappy Sunday traveler, the unlucky ice-cream seeker who was expecting a smile or a "good day" from the officer running "routine traffic stops" but got cuffs instead.

What to do? I'll speak to the first-timer now, to whom any time in any jail cell for any reason can feel like the whole damned world crashing down on their heads. Don't panic! If the warrant that landed you in that holding cell was signed, sealed, and delivered for a simple "failure to appear," you're gonna be okay, Chicken Little. Hell, now you've even got a mug shot, which might score you a wild date or two with a rebellious young hottie if you put it on your Farmers Only profile.

The good news, for some—if a bench warrant went out because you flaked on a misdemeanor and bail was low—kind-hearted judges may just lift that sucker off your shoulders and clear the bail. There's a bit of a wrinkle with this good news: it really helps if a lawyer comes to court for you or with you, if this is what you want done.

Even with something the justice system views as simple and relatively minor as a bench warrant, a sharp

DON'T GO TO JAIL!

attorney can be a lifesaver. We'll find out if there should have been a warrant in the first place, or if the cop who plucked you from your Subaru did everything right. Arrests have been thrown out of court for constitutional violations, rights not being read, you name it. Even brand-new criminal defense attorneys can pull apart the details of a misdemeanor arrest and get it thrown out of court. We live for that shit; it's our Sudoku or Angry Birds or what have you.

Talking about this stuff can be a real downer for anyone, so I try to top the turd sundae with a cherry of hope. No, bench warrants aren't always a big deal in the grand scheme of things, and an unusually savvy average citizen might be able to get out of them. The good news? If the idea of hiring an attorney whose face is on billboards all over town—no matter how handsome that face is—sends visions of being broke and homeless shuffling through your head, you're still in luck. For a fraction of the fees charged by independent counsel, city public defenders can often handle this sort of thing just fine. It's their bread and butter.

They say that 80 percent of success is just showing up. If you remember one thing from our little chat, remember that 100 percent of avoiding bench warrants is *also* just showing up.

So You Had Drugs in Your Car?

America is beginning to see the light, hallelujah! The white-hot lights on fine green ganja in grow houses everywhere, that is. Some states have finally legalized marijuana for medical use, others for playtime. Even in places where the lava lamp hasn't been fully lit in the cobwebbed minds of lawmakers, marijuana laws have been reduced to misdemeanors—we're talking a ticket and you can mosey off to wake-and-bake another day. A tiny $200 ticket! The guys convicted under harsh drug penalties in place a couple of decades ago salute you from the federal pens where they're doing life for a few ounces of Chocolope or Purple Urkle.

Getting pulled over in your beat-down pickup with a couple of baggies of combustible green stowed in the wheel well can end up causing a lot of hassle for the everyday stoner.

Let's take Nebraska as an example of a state that hasn't seen the way, the truth, the light. Our buddies at the National Organization for the Reform of Marijuana Laws (NORML) inform me that if you're found with a small amount of choice Bruce Banner's bellybutton lint there—up to one pound—the top misdemeanor charge could be a minimal fine and a few months in jail.

True captains of industry carting bushels of more than one pound of fine Thelonious Skunk across the Cornhusker State might end up bunking for the next five years in the county's least hospitable bed-and-breakfast, not to mention on the hook for a $10,000 fine.

As long as peace-loving Parrotheads in forty of these fifty great states are still going away for years at a time just because they left the Jimmy Buffett concert early and had the bad luck to run into a routine DUI checkpoint, strategies for handling the harshest buzzkill available are necessary.

"MAN, IT'S NOT JUST WEED"

Okay, this is where a certain pucker factor creeps in. Even though there are plenty of places where the laws treat weed the same as much more troublesome products like coke, meth, or heroin, there are many states that categorize them separately. Some of what I'm about to tell you applies to any drugs found stuffed in a crack in the upholstery. Some is focused only on coping with a measly weed bust. We'll have a sidebar on the heavy stuff.

This is valuable counsel for the price of a decent steak, so consider copying some points I make as we go onto a laminated card to keep in your wallet or your car—it's good to have something in arm's reach when the cops flick on the bullhorn and start practicing their dominance role-play routine outside the bedroom.

IN GENERAL

- **Don't agree to searches.** Like a steadfast Creationist whose daughter's teacher wants to take her on a field trip to the Museum of Evolution: *do not consent*. Once you have, you've given the cops all they need to slingshot you directly into the nearest holding cell just as soon as they find a teeny little Ziploc bag of Maui Wowie your friend forgot when he sold you the car a year ago. The search could still happen whether you agree to it or not, depending on state laws, but any defense you might mount in court will be stronger if you confirm you did not agree to the patrolman's desire to paw through the discarded Taco Cabeza bags in your backseat.
- **Clearly ask if you can go.** No mumbling, no coughing—cops aren't telepathic, so you better enunciate like you're reciting the Pledge of Allegiance at Madison Square Garden. They like it when you say "yes" to searches, so they will press harder if you don't. You might be asked to wait, to build as much tension as possible so you snap and

give in. At some point, they may threaten to call in drug-sniffing dogs. They might do all of this to cover for the fact that they have no old-fashioned "reasonable suspicion" to make you stick around.

"Reasonable suspicion" is "probable cause's" lazy cousin and the heart of why cops stop and hold suspects in the first place. The beauty of refusing a search? It's *not evidence*. As damning as it might feel to refuse, it's nowhere near as damning as evidence that can be used against you. Ask Officer Clodhopper, "Am I free to go and continue living my life as a law-abiding citizen with an outstanding balance on my cable bill and incipient case of psoriasis?" If the answer is "yes," get the hell out of there without going one mile per hour above the speed limit. If the reply is "no," that means they've found a reason to hold you, and you've got a front-row ticket to the Judge-and-Jury sketch show. Even then, don't freak out: the cops will have to defend the arrest. It won't matter if they can trot out that stale Kush as evidence you are keeping the spirit of *Reefer Madness* alive in society today—if you asked to leave before their search began, you may be able to argue that they illegally detained you, and flush their evidence straight down the porcelain highway.

SIDEBAR

I've talked you through some basic principles here and they apply to any similar situation, regardless of the chemical amusements—I could also call them "alternate fuel sources"—and now it's time we face the big stuff. It's time for some tough love.

Like I told you about Nebraska, there are still more places than not where weed will get you in plenty of trouble. If the cops turn up evidence that you're chasing the dragon or mainlining white lady, it can get Afterschool Special–serious. Take meth, for example . . .

Nazis were the first to lean on meth, for its jackhammer stimulation and impressive extension of wakefulness. (Because—Sure! Why not give The Rancor 'roid rage? What could possibly go wrong there?) It was quick to be taken off the legal market, perhaps because it's highly addictive, the process of cooking it up is deadly, and there are too many specific physical ramifications to the user and passersby to list. Even though it's murder on the body—a *Day of the Triffids* level beast of a drug that can dig holes in your brain, face, and teeth—you might find the long arm of the law much more sympathetic to the monkey on your back if it isn't named Meth. No one on the straitlaced side of the law likes it, and they *really* don't like tweakers.

As with weed, there are variations across the country in how badly you'll be nailed if all the measures mentioned in this section fail, and the next thing you know you are trying to convince Johnny Q. Lawman that the crystalline stuff is just rock salt.

(continued)

To put it delicately, you could be boned, filleted, and garnished with a twist of lemon.

An example of just how screwed: Illinois's laws on meth possession alone dictate that just a paltry fifteen grams—half an *ounce* in case the metric system is alien speak to you—is felony possession and will net you a smooth $200,000 fine and up to fifteen years in prison.

Not to mention the delights of shuddering through withdrawal once the cell doors have been locked.

I'm not your dad (I hope), probably not even your lawyer—yet—just a friendly voice here, but penalties for meth, coke, morphine, heroin, or LSD are similar wherever you are. The best bet is to stay the hell away from anything to do with meth and all the rest. As far away as you can possibly get.

- **Refresher: don't agree to a search, and then ask if you can go.**
- **Cops admire the forthright.** Don't do that. We like to think of ourselves as good people. We want to be helpful. The worst time to be a good, helpful person is when you are sweating out the curious gaze of a cop who sees you as the best way to beat the boredom of another shift shuffling papers and watching *Murder, She Wrote* on his cruiser's laptop. Pot feels like small change legally so it might be tempting to drop the dime on yourself—as in,

"Oh, yes, officer, my friend did indeed deposit a gallon freezer bag full of dank in my trunk for safe-keeping, but I assure you I don't partake."

No.

The cops will act as if it's fine, no big deal, buddy, because the law is on their side—it's perfectly okay for them to lie to you. They can befuddle and trick you to their hearts' content, providing whatever cops you're dealing with still have hearts. You need to stay calm and quiet. Be Harold Lloyd with the composure of the Fonz. There's no need to be rude or even get upset. If it feels like the situation is escalating regardless, invoke your right to an attorney and zip it.

- **Most important—this can't be stressed enough—avoid attention in the first place.** It's tempting to the young and invulnerable to test theories like, "Maybe cops will assume this brown roach at the end of this alligator clip is some stylish hipster cigarette." They won't. They won't mistake that glowing cloud of sinsemilla around your head for a halo. Even in legal weed states, getting high *in public* may be illegal. As funny as it is to politely greet an officer with fragrant clouds billowing from your car window, toking up where you can be seen—including inside your car on a public road—is an open invitation to the police to take charge of your agenda and enhance your diet with jail-provided Nutraloaf.

This is the part you can print out, as suggested earlier. It can't hurt, right?

Don't consent to search requests.
Ask if you are free to get the hell out of Dodge.
Shut up.
Save it for home, where the police presence is—
   hopefully—negligible.

Locked Up and Loaded

Man, Orson Welles. Many of us remember him from his days prior to pushing frozen peas and cheap wine and playing bit parts in Muppet flicks. Youngsters take note: the guy made some great films. *The Third Man*, for example. Orson as Harry Lime, a black marketer peddling watered-down meds in Vienna after World War II. Ol' Harry wasn't a gentleman, but the guy had respectable gab. One line is worth repeating here, even though it loses a little something if you can't hear it in Orson's stentorian tones: "In Italy for thirty years under the Borgias they had warfare, terror, murder, and bloodshed, but they produced Michelangelo, Leonardo da Vinci, and the Renaissance. In Switzerland they had brotherly love—they had five hundred years of democracy and peace, and what did that produce? The cuckoo clock."

It's a hard old world out here for most of us, and it's a fact of life that in this world, no one needs a concealed carry license to haul around a cuckoo clock.

The world is still designed for the Borgias, not the clockmakers.

So . . . guns.

It'd be easy to lose ourselves in the tall grass hunting down all the variations in gun laws that allow walking around with a rifle slung over your shoulder in one state and penalize pellet gun owners in another. We have to stick to the big picture here, so I'll whittle it down into a nice chestnut whistle.

Due to the Second Amendment establishing the right of just about any homeowner to keep a musket hung above the fireplace on the rack of a strong buck, it's a given non-felons can own firearms in every state in the Union. The individual states, though, are all over the place when it comes to where you can go with and how you can carry that blunderbuss.

In the great state of Texas, for example, a legal handgun owner with no Texas Concealed Handgun License can still keep their shooter concealed in a boat or car.

Drive west to California and it's a different ball of wax. Want to buy a nice little snubnose .32 Colt just for some home defense? In the Golden State, you will have to present a valid driver's license, proof of residency, and either already have a Handgun Safety Certificate or be able to demonstrate that you're safety-savvy in the presence of your potential piece.

In practice, attorneys don't always deal with the violent side of guns. Sure, we get defendants saddled with murder raps, robbery, or improper exhibition of a firearm outside a particularly antagonistic paintball game, but the bulk of what we see are people trying to have a good time, just blowing off steam, y'know? Maybe they just haven't bothered to bone up on the laws of the land. The following is a little education and advisory for those readers—people who meant no harm, who were just having fun, who didn't know that sometimes it might not be okay to whip it out and fill public property, private vehicles, or inaudible fast-food drive-through speakers with lead.

TARGET PRACTICE

Maybe you're young, dumb, and strapped with Dad's .357 Magnum, going wild down I-40. No one's getting robbed or shot just for the hell of it—you're no *psycho*, you're just exercising *carpe noctem* with your pals. Up ahead is an exit sign. It bears bullet holes from past party animals, so hey, why not? Fire off a few. Maybe your buddies peer-pressured you into showing off your eagle-eye aim . . . and that's exactly when the staties' lights start a-blazin'.

Nothing too dramatic happens—no shoot-out, you just get pulled over and hit with, let's say, unlawful discharge of a firearm. Or illegal use! Or being negligent! What happens next will really be determined by where it occurred (in our example, an interstate), time (night here, when all the youngish rascals are getting their ya-yas out), and how it happened—as in, was it accidental? Threatening? A demonstration of this fine bit of American guncraft's perfect balance gone awry?

Law enforcement takes guns pretty seriously, given how often they end up on the wrong end of one. So it's a hard fact that this won't be a situation in which you should even conceive of defending yourself (see Part I: How to Be Your Own Attorney, "Why You Shouldn't Be Your Own Attorney").

Good news, or at least not-terrible news is, there are several lines of defense most attorneys will consider bringing to the court to hopefully get you out of this jam so you can ride again. . . . But maybe keep the gun at home next time, Rambo.

These lines of defense include, but aren't limited to:

- **You didn't mean to!** "Honestly, I was sure it was unloaded, I stuck it out the passenger window to test my hypothesis that my Magnum is less aerodynamic than my friend's S&W Bodyguards 380—it was for the love of science!" That's the don't-try-this-in-real-life dialogue version, but you get the gist. Another factor: the friends who were supposed to be so impressed, aka witnesses. If it's a tight bunch we're talking about and everyone can square their stories in the time it takes for troopers to draw down and order everyone out of the car—because when gunfire is involved, they will not take chances—by the time the gang's all safe and sound in one of the state patrol's twelve-shades-of-beige interview rooms, they all know for a fact that *no one* knew the gun was loaded. So just like that, the prosecutor will have a heck of a time making the case. The problem here might be that you had the gun with you in the first place, but if the only thing at issue was damage to state property, things will probably turn out okay.

- **Self-defense!** Unlawful random discharge while flying down the road at night as self-defense? Unless your attorney can convince the court you'd spotted a flying purple people eater from Area 51 shooting otherworldly lasers at you and your fellow earthlings, that won't fly. In other situations, though, self-defense might work. Depends on whether you have a buddy in the car whom you'd like to spring an assault charge on, which I do not recommend. It's a bad idea to lie to get friends arrested. Makes things real awkward at the next Friendsgiving potluck.

- **Here's another juicy fact that could potentially fall in your corner: if arresting officers did not see exactly who pulled that trigger, there essentially is no case.** So if there're a few of you riding, pass that thing around to confuse the issue further.

If you're somewhere else, say, cruising along Farmer McFriendly's acreage, randomly popping inanimate objects, your defense may also include "I was on private property." But you better be sure McFriendly's gonna tell the boys in blue that you had his permission to be here. Trespassing with a weapon isn't quite like that stroll in the sunny park I was describing earlier.

Most of us aren't big fans of no-win situations. Convictions can happen, though. If the court decides you totally didn't mean to blast that gun, or intended no harm, you might end up with just a misdemeanor. I'm not saying that's a great scenario. It could be a year in jail, depending on the state you're in. Plus fines and perhaps repair of whatever damage was done.

It's pretty easy to sum this up: don't shoot stuff if you don't have permission to. And if you're going to be brandishing a firearm about willy-nilly, make sure you keep the safety on.

Is That a Gun in Your Pocket or Are You Just Happy to Meet the TSA?

Traveling isn't the same as it once was. There was a time, a wonderful time, when you could breeze through a quick scan at airport security before enjoying a cigarette and a scotch while a musician tickled the ivories at the plane's piano bar.

Now there's a Great Wall of scanning technology and civil servants who know how much you hate it when they put their gloved hands where the sun don't shine. This wall is under control of the Transportation Security Administration, and thousands upon thousands of people get through them every day with very little incident, save a few unpleasant tingles.

Now and then, though, someone who packed too fast at home gets their navy blue dress socks mixed up with their Glock. It happens. I mean, I'm sure it's happened once, somewhere. Maybe they keep the piece protected by that Italian wool so that it doesn't get scratched up. Anyhow, they jog off to the airport, not a care in the world, wait patiently in line to meet the fine folks of the TSA, shuck off their shoes, put their carry-on on the X-ray scanner, and—oh, boy. There's that Glock, not those Bill Blass socks. It's glowing white-hot on the scanner and everyone in line is staring at you, the unlucky traveler who accidentally sent a firearm through.

If you've seen news stories about this, you know it happens to perfectly normal people all the time. What follows?

There is a whole menu of charges available to a hungry prosecutor presented with a wayward gun found by the TSA. One simple charge might be "concealing a weapon without a concealed carry permit." That's a few thousand in fines and maybe a year in jail. But wait, there's more! There's also the fact the weapon was carried into a known restricted area, and that's an additional misdemeanor worth 180 days in lockup and a few more thousand dollars' worth of "whoopsy."

Worst-case? Ten years in jail and a $10,000 fine on a felony count of carrying a concealed weapon. Might as well be aware of just how deep that particular shithole goes.

What kind of case will your poor attorney face when he walks into court, full of youth and energy and ready to fight for justice? The prosecutor may be pushing to prove, above all else, that you really meant to do that. They'll look for proof you tucked that gun away with *some* kind of ill intent. It's not pretty, which is why you and your counsel need to convince the court there's no way you'd intentionally do such a thing. It was early in the morning. It was really late at night, and you just wanted your nice socks.

There are, should you need to know them, perfectly legal ways to travel with your gun. They don't involve acting like you thought it was socks. The TSA says, first of all, if you're going somewhere that has regulations against carrying a firearm, don't bring the damned thing along at all. The English, for example, won't allow their rooty-tooty shooty cousins across the ocean to bring hot lead injectors onto their clammy soil.

If heading to a destination where people find it perfectly copacetic for you to have a little Winchester-provided protection, then simply declare every single bullet, pin, and barrel part of your equipment as you're checking in, long before you reach the TSA. Make sure you're a licensed owner when you do it.

There are clear guidelines for properly packing your

piece on the TSA's website, TSA.gov. Recap: learn how to pack your piece to avoid the police.

Other Peoples' Guns

What if you get pulled over for a normal traffic infraction, maybe just ten miles over the speed limit, and—God forbid—you accidentally agree to a search? And then, even worse, what if that search turns up a firearm, and it's not yours? This kind of thing happens all the time.

That whole "possession is nine-tenths of the law thing" sums it up nicely. If it's in your possession, in your car, in your care, it don't matter if you're looking after the musket of Christopher Columbus himself—if it's under your watch, you'd better be able to prove that Chris transferred the registration over to you.

If the gun is in your vehicle—or home, or locker at work, you get the picture—and some kind of police search determines it isn't yours, well, it can get pretty hairy, pretty fast.

Hey, maybe you borrowed it! Or, more likely, it was given to you. Plenty of moms and dads bequeath all kinds of property to their beloved kids and grandkids in wills with little concern for whatever legal wrinkles arise. Say gramps left you his lucky Smith & Wesson .22. Its serial number was registered in his name. You—overcome with grief over losing your doting Pops—don't bother to register said pistol with the authorities. Also, maybe work takes you through a bad part of town. So when you return, still sad but picking up the pieces after grampa's funeral, you see that well-cared-for old gun and decide to give it a ridealong.

If that serial number comes up in a police database search, some suspicious parties may come to the conclusion that it's been stolen. Now it's time to ask the $64 question: did we know it was considered stolen?

Of course not, what a dumb question. That's why it's only worth $64. But it is the question that matters here. The law tends to believe if you *know* you've got some hot iron in hand, there was intent to reap some benefit for you, or for potentially anyone other than the actual owner of the weapon. Prosecutors will try a case if they think they can kick reasonable doubt right in the balls by proving these key things:

- **The person with the gun in hand at the time of arrest knew in the moment that they had a stolen gat.**
- **That person was somehow going to benefit from the stolen property.** Maybe by selling it and using the

profits to buy a turntable for their scratch-happy cat, or selling it and funneling the money back to whomever took it in the first place.

So . . . your takeaway? It'll serve you well (and you'll be less likely to serve time) if you show the good folks of the court that you had no idea the gun in your possession would be considered stolen property. Because you didn't. It's important to remember, in this case, that you don't know shit. Furthermore, you were doing what you were doing out of the goodness of your ever-good heart; there were no benefits to you from this property.

Speaking of stolen property, let's move along to that sparkly shipment of gadgets that fell off a truck before a certain Good Samaritan (your friend, let's say) did a respectable public service by selling the gadgets on the cheap last holiday season.

"Possession" can be like beauty: the definition's in the eyes of the beholder. No matter the smart-sounding definition, possession has some big legal muscles with perpetual flex power. Read on to aim that flex power at your "friend's" foes.

It's Not Your Fault
Your Friends Steal

We've all got that one friend. They just love playing the perennial Santa Claus, seeing their friends' faces light up when they bring them the perfect book or record or carving knife set for no occasion at all. I had a pal, let's call her Tiffany, who brought me a snazzy new tie every time we met up for a late-night Moscow Mule. Tiffany had impeccable taste, but this sugar-sweet gal had a serious problem. She was a grade-A fingersmith, and not the type you ask for at a full-service massage parlor. She lifted stuff. It started off as an altruistic little thrill to provide her hardworking friends and family with a little something extra just because, but then it spun off into a full-blown addiction. Sure, maybe some folks realize they can make a fair chunk of change from re-selling their ill-gotten goods on eBay or Etsy or in the 7-Eleven parking lot or whatever, but most thieves—if they're honest—get a real kick out of taking other peoples' stuff. Who needs roller coasters when you've got the rush of sidling out of an electronics store, winking at the loss prevention goons so that they don't notice the MP3 player tucked neatly inside your waistband? Long ago, when some drugstores stocked the skin mags right there with *Field & Stream* and not far from *Today's*

Bride, I knew of a guy who never once left a store of that type without his jacket stuffed with copies of *Penthouse* or *Oui* or—if he was moving too fast—*Family Handyman.* No one ever turned him in because he was always willing to share, and he was the only one on the block who knew how to replace the splash guard on a garbage disposal.

One thing some thieves learn early in their career is that their friends often make the best fences or provide the best storage facilities. This is how enabling your harmless shoplifter buddy can turn a good, mall-shopping, lotto-playing American like you into a criminal.

If this were a college course, I'd call it "Intro to Practical Consideration of Perspectives on Receiving Stolen Property." I'd slot it at a convenient time, just after the cafeteria serves those fresh cinnamon buns, but not early enough to make you night owls compromise your beauty rest. I'd forego a final exam, pending student participation. I woulda made a helluva professor— motivation and enthusiasm and showmanship for days. But that's another book entirely.

All this to say, handling a sticky legal situation is often as much about the point of view you approach it with as it is about the alleged crime itself. Having a blue-shirted brigade come knocking on your door with a wake-up warrant for theft is serious business, but what if your perspective all along is, "Hey, man—of course this isn't my stuff"? Sometimes your smartest move is playing dumb. You want to be an accessory? Romance a dowager countess and while away your days comfortably in the south of France sipping champagne like all good arm candy.

I'll give a hypothetical to make things clear: let's say your good buddy White Dice pulls up to your house with a van full of electronic gear and instruments. A complete rock band setup.

"Wow," you think, "old Dice is tone-deaf! Not to mention, he lost half a finger in a smelting accident a few years back! Why is he starting a band?"

White Dice asks if he can store the stuff in your garage until he gets a chance to set up a rehearsal space, and you say yes, because Andrea Bocelli was no spring chicken when he got his big break—who's to say it's too late for your pal to drop the heavy machinery and take up a career in heavy metal?

Plus, White Dice has had some rough times lately, so at the very least it's good for him to have a hobby. Maybe he's learning to drum? He can definitely hold a pair of sticks, and they don't need to be able to differentiate musical notes as long as they can keep up with the tempo, right? Maybe this will lead to something! You should probably start making T-shirts and prepping a tour bus now.

While you're getting lost in the possibilities, White Dice drives off. A few mornings later, the doorbell rings and it isn't the Dice Man! It's a theft and fraud detective, maybe a pair of them, and they want to talk to you about your friend.

Sitting in your garage is gear owned by—I don't know—The Bonky Honky Tonky or somebody like that. Biggest three-piece band in the southwest. In the county. Or maybe they're just the biggest garage band at Turkey Hill Middle School. It doesn't matter, what's important is that you've *received stolen property*.

The sunny-side up version of what might happen next is: you say you didn't know the stuff was stolen, and when the detectives nab White Dice, he corroborates your story and admits you didn't know. And that's that—you're good to go. I mean, it won't be quite that simple, of course, but it might be pretty close.

Now, let's be pessimistic. We need to imagine worst-case scenarios because knowing just how badly things can go wrong is how you develop a contingency plan. Sure, there will probably be blue skies and puffy clouds on the day a hundred of your friends and fam show up for your Independence Day dream wedding. But don't end up cursing your stars—rent that expensive gazebo canopy in case a freak July blizzard turns your beachy vows into a blustery marital botch. So what's the summer snowstorm scenario got to do with the liberated instruments stacked between your lawn mower and those six boxes of term papers in your garage?

Look: it's not illegal to be the person who gets saddled with stolen goods if you didn't know they were stolen.

However, let's say you decide to make a statement and it goes a little like this: "Honest, officers, I did not know that White Dice was creeping around the BHT at the Git-Fiddle Ho-down Show. I didn't know he'd stolen anything. I promise, I thought he was starting a band, or taking an interest in equipment repair." (I'm assuming that you are quick enough on your feet to not mention knowing our hypothetical pal totally has a tin ear.)

Prosecutors could say White Dice went to the venue to steal that equipment. That was his intent all along. He knew he could do it and then hide the gear because he had a buddy—that's you—who was willing to provide the storage space.

To make things worse: if they question enough people, they might find out White Dice is tone-deaf anyway. As his friend, they'll take the big leap of assuming you knew this. Hopefully you can see where I'm headed here. Now you're on the hook for felony accessory to theft charges, when your only real crime was having a garage. And being a supportive friend.

So: where did things go wrong? Should you cut ties with your friends and family, put up a big fence and train a guard dog to chase off everyone but the post-woman? No, it wasn't doing a favor for your friend that got you into trouble; it was giving that statement to the police.

Sometimes even what feels like the most straight-forward, innocent statement can and will be used against you in a court of law. That's why I want to put into your brain a Mormon Tabernacle Choir of Saul Goodmans singing "MAKE NO STATEMENTS" to the tune of the "Hallelujah Chorus."

As soon as the notion "the cops want to talk to me about a thing and they might think I'm involved" flits like a butterfly between your ears—ask for a lawyer. They'll make sure you don't say anything that might make you sound complicit in illegal activities.

And this should be clear, but just in case: it's best to never knowingly deal with stolen goods. If you do know-ingly deal with them, I'd guess you're making some money at it. And if you are putting away some sweet tax-free coin flipping ill-gotten goods snatched from touring rock band trailers—put a criminal defense attorney on retainer, Robin Hood. You'll need one.

Shoplifting or Thrifty Acquisition?

Now that we've cleared your name from second-hand involvement in those hypothetical crimes committed by other people, let's imagine what might happen if you find yourself tempted to take a five-finger discount on an especially seductive jar of exfoliating sugar scrub.

Ah, the venerable pastime of shoplifting. If we traveled back in time to markets in ancient cities whose names now only appear in Julius Caesar's memoirs, we would be able to spot someone with a slightly oversized toga slipping between the stalls and grabbing goods real fast and quiet, never paying a single drachma.

There are a few crimes that folks who'd never even dare to jaywalk can understand, and I think shoplifting's one of them. That doesn't mean it's excusable in the eyes of the law, but it does mean some shoplifters aren't thieves seeking a thrill or resellers scoring new stock— they're honest citizens clinging to the final frayed ends of their ropes. It's just too damned easy sometimes to walk into even the most minor retail establishment, check the dusty wasteland of your wallet, and realize just how much you suddenly covet and *need* some of that stuff around you. Slim Jims never looked so tasty as when you couldn't even muster the measly $2.99 to buy them.

And sometimes shoplifters have no idea they're

shoplifting at all. It's hard to believe, but it *has* happened! Take a trip with me to fantasy-land. . . .

It's hot out. Desert hot. You decide to invest in some bottled water because there's not a Brita filter in the world strong enough to filter the taste of your rusty pipes out of the natural liquid flowing from the tap. It may not be good for the environment, but it's your life—you make the choices. You head to the grocery store, grab a flat of twenty-four bottles, and stick it under the cart.

At the checkout all the rigmarole of loading the belt, handing the cashier your discount card, eyeing the cute bagger distracts you, and you forget that case of bottled water on the bottom rung of the cart. Everyone misses it, including the cute bagger, because you're too busy chatting him up, trying to see if he's single.

Feeling pretty flush from this stimulating conversation, you head for the automatic doors. Next thing you know, store security is there! Belt tight under bulging belly, crew-cut hairs needle-sharp. Loss Prevention wants to know what you were doing with that twenty-four-pack, pardner.

"I didn't even know I'd missed it," you plead. But it might be too late.

To accuse someone of shoplifting, there is a clear set of conditions that retailers need to meet. They need the same thing cops need (one reason among many ex-cops or moonlighting current cops are often the guys and gals following customers down the aisles and giving them the old stink eye—they're used to keeping this stuff in mind): our ancient enemy, "probable cause." Officer Unforgiving, star member of the store's security squad, establishes probable cause when he believes he's seen you hide an item in some way: pockets, bag, or—if he's trying to stretch things because you were wearing a Johnny Cash shirt and he thinks The Man in Black is overrated— the bottom of the cart. He then has to have tracked your journey to the exit, watched you not get that item scanned at checkout, and catch you leaving the store.

We're dealing with a fascinating situation here. It's a little like the store is, for a minute or two, its own sovereign nation. Security guards know and love this. So what could very well happen in this moment is that the definition of probable cause could be stretched like a medieval mischief maker on a torture rack. The guard confronting you is assuming you were trying to steal that water, and he'll also assume you may not know your rights. Which, again, is a thing enforcers can do in-store and out. This assumption will be used to make an ass out of you. The guard may even have a phone at the ready to dial 911 at the first inkling of trouble.

And our fine union perpetuates a common legal hiccup: variations in statutes are different from one state to the next. In one, a cop may laugh off the stray case of bottled water. In another, everyone will absolutely assume you concealed that H_2O by choice and slap you with a shoplifting charge. I've seen cute little grannies get small jail time for stray tins of cat food that slipped beneath their big moth-eaten purses in the shopping cart while rich businessmen who accidentally "test-drive" cars for a month might have the vehicles recovered without charge, fodder for a story between the fellas at the next tee time.

You want to know why I'm focusing on this brand of petty theft at all? Two tiny but incredibly crucial words to the maintenance of your personal liberty: "wiggle room." That idea that the letters of the law are all practicing yogis, and they've become pretty darn flexible. I use this elasticity to get folks out of trouble all the time, but the law bends both ways. Legal wiggle room can help prosecutors slap extra charges on just about any menu, and it can permit police to hold you for a period of time without filing charges. Even this small-time offense can escalate quickly if the heat's turned up to the right degree.

But, back to your grocery store dilemma: if the valiant guardian of the cold cuts and the dairy aisles convinces you to return to the store to clear things up, they are acting reasonably. But one thing you should know is that store security can't keep you locked in a starkly lit room with the flop sweat of a thousand past shoplifters hanging in the air. If they think they've got probable cause and notify the police, they can keep you in the store proper and track you as you wait for the cops to show, but they can't limit you to their cell of shame. So, if you wanted, you could just wander around being watched, if it makes you feel less anxious. Or if you're into that sort of thing.

The important thing now is—whatever the truth was, whether you really were stealing or not—you have the

SIDEBAR

In this situation or one like it, it may be smart to gauge just how convinced your accuser is—I've put forward a scene where security approaches a suspected shoplifter directly, but it's just as likely to be a regular store clerk. If they don't mention bringing in the cops right away, be proactive and invoke them yourself. It's an admirably ballsy move that might make them back off, or it might double the time it takes for you to get a citation or get straight-up arrested. Go big or go home, right? Here's hoping your accusers don't want to deal with all that nonsense, and you simply get to go home. Best case, they just want their organic honey roasted tofurkey slices back, and to believe it was all a mis-understanding. And in that case, you will comply.

right to keep your mouth shut. Your rights are the same in this commercial dystopia as they are in the real world, so your best bet might be not to say anything.

"Saul!" I hear you squeal. "That's as good as admitting I was doing something as lame as stealing bottled water!"

That may be, but take the long view, Sparky. The inalienable right to not incriminate yourself in any circumstance remains. And really, trying to reason your way out of some hullabaloo may just end badly here.

Summation

You'd be surprised at how easy it might be to war-game all the shit that could go down if you've been caught stealing, even once. Maybe that'll be my next book title: *The Shit That Could Go Down*. I'll try to keep it simple here with a few things to remember about shoplifting, if it happens to you:

- **A cool head can equal the upper hand.** Stitch that into a sampler. Tattoo it on your knuckles. In very small print, I guess. Anyway, see the previous sidebar. Humans aren't geared toward eternal conflict. Sometimes, though it can seem otherwise, people just want to get along with the least possible fuss. Dialing the drama back is the smart move in many situations, like here. Show some humility. Treat it as a simple misunderstanding between people of good intentions and see where that goes. If it goes straight to hell, jump the Good Ship Understanding and see the next point.

- **Don't go berserk about your constitutional rights when retail staff first stops you.** On that score, the Fourth Amendment's protection from unreasonable searches and seizures doesn't apply until the cops show up. The innocent and the damned alike might rage against the lying of the clerks, or the guards, or whomever. The innocent want to because they are, of course, innocent. The damned do it because it's a natural reaction to try and cover your ass by acting as the wounded party. Like when Janice in Accounting didn't invite you to her birthday hootenanny and you went around telling everyone that you wouldn't have gone to that yawnfest anyway. It doesn't do either of you any good. The employees'll think the lady doth protest too much, and all that jazz. Wait for your attorney to show up—we'll be the megaphone voicing your injustice so you don't have to strain your larynx right into a public disturbance charge.

- **When the cops arrive, shut up, if you haven't already.** This is the broken record portion of the festivities. Not to deal in redundancy, but: seriously, shut up. Lawyers do the talking from here on out. In fact, if the "we're all reasonable people" approach I've mentioned fails miserably and you wind up in that dark little room next to where security people pretend to play Customer Pac-Man with their video surveillance equipment, they may try some very cop-like shit (because, as you remember from earlier, they are often cops when they clock out into the daylight). You could be told if you just fill out a statement regarding what happened, the cops don't have to get involved and this won't become some big, messy, legal to-do. All these folks do is nab retail rustlers all day. Don't do it.

- **This isn't a total disaster. Truth is, shoplifting is a petty crime.** There's a good chance you won't be driven away in a squad car at all, just given a citation—though that does depend on where you are and how vindictive the store personnel is feeling, not to mention how sick they are of this kind of shit in the first place. If they've been having a big problem preventing loss, they might take the hardline and make an example of you. But even then, the charge usually only jumps to felony level if the accused was trying to tiptoe half the store away.

Penalties for shoplifting vary widely depending on where you are. Some states specify that there is *no* jail time at all if the dollar value of the stolen goods is relatively small. A pilfered case of bottled water might end up costing a few hundred in fees and fines, but no time on the inside.

Still—if I'm going to spend that much on water, it better cure cancer or be bottled straight out of the Fountain of Youth. Your best bet is to just follow the commandments, and try not to steal. If you suffer a moment of weakness and you get caught: shut up and lawyer up.

Driving Under the Influence of Fun!

I'm not one to judge (it's not in my job description—at least not yet), but there's nothing funny about driving under the influence of anything. Driving while drunk is incredibly stupid, irresponsible, and potentially deadly. For you, and everyone in your path. Driving stoned isn't any better, no matter how mellow it feels or how enlightened you think you are.

And yet, short-sighted people do it all the time. DUIs, OUIs, anything-you-can-think-of-UIs could be any given defense attorney's stock-in-trade, the main thing they do all day. They present a slew of challenges, because irresponsible behavior is so tied up with the diminished-capacity side effect of sipping liquid courage. It's very tricky to prove your client's innocence. Let's keep the hopeful thought that if you, my friend, are guilty of driving under the influence, it was a special-circumstances one-time-only thing, and you didn't hurt anyone. Everybody makes mistakes, and you deserve the chance to walk free and never, ever repeat your mistakes. Let's take a sobering journey through how this might go down.

THE STOP

Long day at work, huh, champ? Of course a trip to the watering hole was in order. A highly understandable pit stop, an invigorating filling station for your sanity. It's that sweet, necessary chance to take a few deep breaths after the end of a long hard day farming, constructing, accounting, filing, representing clients, whatever your labor. A time to pull yourself together before you return home to the loving spouse, the incontinent pet, or the deafening silence.

You only have one shot of tequila. Okay, only five.

Who's counting? Then you check your watch, pay your tab, and hit the road.

So many things could happen next. It's not unheard of for cops to park and "do paperwork" by various booze dispensaries just so they can swoop in like a lioness scouting for wounded wildebeest out on the African savannah. (Factual reminder, it's actually the lioness who does the hunting for the pride. Respect.) Typically, though, a driver who has had a few might be kind of loosey-goosey, all over the road, too fast then too slow. Maybe your cell phone fell out of your cup holder as you took a turn too quickly and you swerved a bit as you reached down to grab it. A number of conditions inside the car can cause this sort of driving, but yeah, it's usually going to read "rockin' the rotgut" to the cops, and they'll hit the lights before you can straighten the tires.

Pay close attention now, buckaroo. You've been pulled over for weaving or whatever. The officer approaches, you open your window, and you have to just imagine in that moment that the man or woman who flagged you is Robocop, with the red computer display on the bottom of their visual field. It's ticking off a few things cops are trained to look for:

- **The old classic: slurred speech.** Plenty of drunk folks can cope with that and speak with great clar-

ity, though they might as well be reciting the Jab-
berwocky, for all the sense their well-enunciated
words make when strung together.

- **Leaky, red eyeballs.** One of the dead giveaways,
  and it can occur in several different breeds of
  messed up.

- **Shitty coordination.** Maybe you take too long digging your ID out of your wallet. Or flop around
  like a fish freshly plopped on a boat deck as you
  lean over to grab the registration from the glove
  box. That magic sauce (or dust or smoke or what
  have you) we put in our bodies to cloud our brains
  screws our reflexes by default. Cops learn to look
  for that, and most of them can see through attempts to compensate.

- **The pious confession.** You roll up to the checkpoint unperturbed—you got this. But then maybe
  it's the officer's aggressively over-ironed uniform
  or those suddenly intimidating orange traffic cones
  or maybe you mistake your midnight munchies for
  a pang of conscience . . . something makes you
  fess up and tell the truth. Or a degree of it. "I just
  had two beers, Officer, but it was like several hours
  ago and I'm for sure not drunk." Your smidgeon
  of honesty is enough to help you realize imme-
  diately, as does the officer: you're delivering

yourself to the hellish drunk tank in a proverbial hand basket, this one woven by your own heroic (and stupid) confession. This happens in DUI stops more often than you'd think. Sometimes a little bit of the truth won't go a long way, it'll just get you cuffed.

THE TESTS

One or all the conditions that add up to a possible DUI being met, it's time for tests. Some of which most sober people couldn't pass. I for one cannot hopscotch backward while reciting the states of the union in alphabetical order. I'd wish you luck here, but that's as hopeless as a goldfish headed upstream at Niagara Falls. So you likely fail this sobriety test miserably.

Good news, sort of! In many places, field sobriety tests are elective! It may be a good strategy to opt out. Bad news: there will be penalties for refusing the damned thing. And that refusal will probably trigger a reading of the "implied consent" agreement. See, in refusing that test, you've put yourself in a position to choose between two other tests: blood or breath. Refuse a breathalyzer or a blood test? *BAM!* Your license is automatically suspended.

Then comes the arrest portion of the festivities. If you've gotten this far, yes, the government-issued stainless-steel bracelets are coming. Hopefully you've fully digested what I've been feeding you up to this point and have kept your mouth shut. Because if the police have fully established what they consider probable cause—and refusal of any test tends to provide that— then you are about to go for a nice little swim in the drunk tank.

THE NEXT STEP

Now? You are definitely going to need an attorney. The Internet will be your friend here, though many attorneys who specialize in DUI cases are canny enough to put their smiling faces on signs and billboards about town where potential clients might catch sight of them from their backseat tour of the metropolitan district.

A lawyer whose bread and butter is DUI or one who at least is drunk-driving friendly will be able to negotiate the nasty maze of paperwork and procedures. He or she will hopefully be a familiar face at the courthouse, which believe me, can really help sometimes—don't discount your attorney's ability to charm other officers of the court. An attorney who is savvy with DUIs will also know their way around a plea bargain. If you go to court with a DUI charge, especially if it's not your first, you really need that know-how.

If you end up in an attorney's office, a chat will

commence. I'll try to give you a feeling for what that will be like without scaring the whiskey piss out of you.

- **First thing's first: a little homework.** A good number of lawyers endorse this practice: write it down. Become an impassioned, detail-oriented memoirist of your DUI. *A Heartbreaking Work of a Staggering Inebriant, In Cold Booze,* you get the idea. This will be painful; it just will. But it's necessary. And be honest. Chapter one: where were you and what were you doing before you got behind the wheel? Chapter two: how long were you driving, what were you listening to, what Foghat song were you jamming to when you first noticed the disco blue? Were you listening to "Slow Ride" while slowly weaving across the centerline? Map it out in words and know it cold. Name anyone in the car with you. Give your version of the pleasant conversation I'm sure you had with the officer.

  A defendant in this situation needs to be as clear as possible about their perspective because the prosecution has a hooked trident poised to stick in your booze-bloated side now that they've caught you in their net. The prongs are:
    - *Whatever the cops observed about how you were driving when they put on the lights.*

- *Your demeanor and all that stuff about leaky eyes and floppy fish hands with the wallet.*
- *The results of the tests you took, if you did end up taking them.*

- **Second, a caution:** don't conclude you are done, even if you set that breathalyzer on fire with your flaming rum toddy breath. Just because someone blows a certain blood alcohol percentage doesn't necessarily mean they're roasted. Attorneys can question every minute detail. They can bring up the reliability of the breathalyzer machine, for example. Some of those things can have a near 50 percent margin of error! DUIs are not automatic slam dunks for the state every time, no matter how much they believe they are.

- **Every state handles DUI penalties a little differently.** You might be fined. License suspended. Or if the system is in compassionate mode and deems you salvageable from the dominance of old demon rum—and you have a decent attorney, good luck, or both—a treatment program. The consequences will depend on the circumstances. Was it your first time? Just how shit-faced were you? Did you lower your window and promptly ralph half a bowl of cheesy-bacon waffle fries on the officer's shoes, you know, casually? Were you a loud, defensive asshole prior to arrest? All that will factor in.

- **Get in touch with your friendly local DMV or RMV.** They're the same, different states just have different names, and procedures. Here in New Mexico, it's the "MDV," which sounds about 50 percent less funny in punch lines. If it is vital that you be able to drive while awaiting trial, you can go to the MDV, hat in hand, and very meekly ask for an administrative hearing. A lawyer can help you here, let you know what options to seek. Sometimes people waiting for the DUI hammer to drop can get specially restricted licenses that let them drive to work and back. Do not pass go, *do* pass every single bar and liquor store you see.

- **Whatever you do, don't talk about your arrest with anyone.** I know! After a while, it feels like all we lawyers do is tell you to shut up. It's like we want all the words to ourselves. In these situations, we do, because we *know the right words to say.* Shutting the hell up about a DUI is just practical, too. It can affect the way coworkers and bosses discuss you at the water cooler. DUI family theater is even less fun. And anyone you blab to about that night can be called to testify against you in a court of law. Just getting slapped with a DUI charge has you boned enough—don't double down on it by blabbing about it to everyone.

- **This should be obvious at this point, but: don't say a word to anyone in law enforcement without the comforting presence of legal counsel by your side.** Not even a restricted license option available? Do not under any circumstances drive anything. Keep your car in the garage. Hands off the old Segway. Don't even sit on your kid's Big Wheel. No driving, no how. And, you know, for the love of Pete, don't drink and drive *again*.

The Trial

I think I've already touched on many elements that will go into enduring a DUI trial. The prosecution's focus—loopy driving, red eyes; roadside, blood, or breathalyzer tests—and some of the strategies a DUI attorney could employ in their valiant efforts to keep you out of lockup. Your attorney can pick these things apart, maybe try to find reasonable doubt in something as simple as the time elapsed between the moment you were first stopped and when the officer administered the breath test, or whether your blood was refrigerated properly or not before the scientists threw it in the rusty old gas chromatograph. Even in an unsavory crime like a DUI, you remain innocent until the state proves you were drunk as a skunk.

Can you win? Damn, Sunny Jim, it's possible. Here's how:

First, don't even consider pleading guilty. Nope, not even a little, no. The system owes you your damned day in court for this charge—otherwise, what are we even doing on this big blue ball? Just waiting around for another asteroid to strike?

Next, prepare. Client and attorney both need to become legal Rain Men as far as the case is concerned, with detailed, total knowledge of every minor detail. Line up challenges to every possible element: to the tests, to the lab work involving the blood (if blood was drawn to measure alcohol content), to the officer's personal record—you get the picture. Those hardworking folks up in the state house—in pretty much every state—have, under pressure from groups lobbying hard to end drunk driving, stacked the deck of legislation against defendants and defense counsel. So you and your counselor have to be better. Faster. Stronger. Members of my tribe who do go ahead and advertise as specialists in DUI law are up-to-date on hopefully every element of the legislation. We know many cases are more winnable than they seem. It's just good old-fashioned professionalism. You should expect that from the guy who fixes your car, from your favorite erotic dancer, and most definitely from your attorney.

Often a good idea: have your history and head discussed with and checked by a substance-abuse counselor. This can reduce the danger of looking like a potential three-peater—or five-peater—to the prosecutor. It's a way to say, "Hey, I know, I *might* have a wee little problem here." In addition to that assessment, round up medical records. If you've ever had any one of a number of medical challenges, they can have a profound effect on how you responded at the time you were stopped. What if you have a mild learning disability and the officer's instructions during the sobriety tests were hard to follow? How fair is that, to get a DUI for the same reason you once failed PE class? Sure, mean old Coach Thunderthighs from junior high might say "Very fair," but Coach would be wrong.

Act like you're applying to the Ivys and put together the most detailed résumé possible. Academic records— especially if those are halfway decent—verification that you are a solid citizen with a job, proof that you volunteer to read to the kids at the public library every Saturday, anything that makes you look like a modern Mother Teresa who was temporarily blinded by life's injustices and made one stupid mistake. Demonstrating the valuable and positive ways in which you contribute to society matters, because a DUI has a lot of moral and political weight to it. If this is your first DUI, you want to prove you aren't the kind of boozehound who will keep knocking them back long after you've fallen off the bull. If this isn't your first stumble into the rodeo ring, it helps to prove you've seen that you are of value to others and have a lot to lose.

The Sobriety
(Or Something Like It)

Say you win, or the case is thrown out on a technicality— it goes away, somehow, and there are no substantial penalties to you, if any at all. Hooray. Figure out what you did wrong in the first place and don't repeat it. And pay your attorney, because they could use a deep tissue foot massage after the song-and-dance they performed to keep you out of trouble.

Say you lose. We've already covered that, at least a little. Hopefully your attorney has been managing your expectations, because a lawyer who isn't up-front about the shitty outcomes you might be facing isn't giving you the best possible representation. They aren't doing themselves any favors, either, because disillusioned clients are bad for repeat business.

Having said that: there's a chance you won't spend additional time in jail, since first offense DUIs are often misdemeanors. True, that could still mean a whole six months in the clink, and differences in jurisdiction matter a great deal here—but a first arrest won't necessarily result in a ton of jail time. I'd love to reassure you more than that, but every prosecutor has a different little shoulder devil, so the way they leverage the available penalties against you, even if it's your first time, will be a little unpredictable. If your blood alcohol was super high, it will affect the penalty, and if you ran over a kid, a nun, or an unleashed pet, you're pretty boned and will probably face felony penalties.

Very reassuring, I know, like a warm, fuzzy blanket that smells like a corpse. But wait, back to fines. There are fines incurred when you lose a case. Maybe pretty low (think mid-triple-digits), but they'll be coming. The really prickly stuff, the little legal cold sores that are going to keep flaring up for the rest of your life, will be—in addition to having a record—dealing with driver's license issues. Your license might be suspended for as few as ninety days for a first-time booze cruise on the autobahn, and potentially years for repeat customers.

More semi-good news for the freshman at DUI High: plenty of states now provide less jail-happy alternative punishments. These might include treatment programs, antidrug-or alcohol-education-related community service, and restitution (if, God forbid, your DUI was acquired after first responders discovered you stumbling away from some kind of traffic accident).

To brighten your day even further: there will be plenty more fallout from the DUI-Bomb, including difficulties with car insurance—getting any at all, for instance—and the fact that some places won't even hire a job applicant if there's a DUI on your record.

SIDEBAR

This is some gloomy stuff, but I'm going to hold out the hope that you don't need any of this information yet, and maybe it'll make you hesitate a beat before lining up those five kamikaze shots to take the edge off your drive home. Fact is, I want you to have fun! But there are plenty of ways to have fun that don't involve you risking your life and the lives of every evening jogger south of your own personal Bourbon Street. Mini-golf, for example. Or laser tag. I know a guy who can hook you up with a few free rounds, if you're looking to unwind.

Summation

Drinking is a great American pastime and I salute your right to practice it to your heart's content if you so choose! Tip one back for Saul Goodman the next time you darken the door of your favorite Palace of Hooch. But if someone offers to buy you a glass of wine after you've hit your limit? Say "no way, rosé" and drink a glass of water.

Driving after you've guzzled down one too many burning gulps of that Fireball can give you the legal equivalent of gonorrhea, so try to avoid that pain and irritation by taking cabs or utilizing a rideshare service. This is one instance where I'll welcome the business, but kind of wish there was no need for it in the first place.

And if you insist on driving yourself: peel off that "Bottle on Board" bumper sticker, stick some Visine in your glove compartment, maybe invest in one of those portable breathalyzers—even if it's not that accurate, you'll at least appear to have made an effort to not drive under the influence. As always: if the cops pull you over, your first best move is to keep your lips zipped and contact an attorney as soon as you can.

We All Have Needs

Our physical needs and desires are part and parcel with having skin, bones, dopamine receptors, and uvulas (those little waggy thingies that hang in our throats, for you future Ken Jennings out there). It's a fact of life that sometimes, our needs can't be easily, efficiently, fancifully, etc. (depending on the proverbial hole you need filled) addressed at home. An essential as established as human civilization itself—occasionally we just need to be intimate with another warm body. If it requires exchanging money and treating that intimacy as a paid service, maybe that's what rubs your Buddha, or maybe your Aphrodite. . . .

Not shockingly, this nation founded by Puritans has been pretty slow to recognize this exchange as a viable manner of human relations. Outside that paradise of gambling and ghost towns known as the Great State of Nevada, paying someone to partake in a heated match of the horizontal hula tends to remain illegal.

Short of the violence too often inflicted on sex workers by malicious clients, soliciting is a fairly victimless crime for both the client and the companion. But much like a DUI, it can lead to a cruelly enhanced public profile for the unfortunates who get busted for partaking in the oldest profession in the world. "Johns" arrested for the crime of rocking the Cash-Only Casbah can end up with their names and even faces in newspapers.

Let's do a little walk-through of what a solicitation case can be like. Common traps set by law enforcement, how to use those traps to your advantage, how to proceed with your case—here's the whole shebang. Statistically, it's a pretty safe assumption to believe that if you've landed in this solicitation snafu from the client side, you're probably of the male disposition. That's not to say that ladies don't have needs—I can't even count the many and varied combinations of bedfellows that money can buy—but this example is going to stick with the plain vanilla male client/female provider scenario.

HOOK, LINE, AND SINKER

Most legal terminology is more confusing than a barking cat. Words heard in other parts of life take on shades of meaning that confuse and torture non-lawyers. "Solicitation" is that kind of word. Like, a guy who shows up at your door trying to sell magazine subscriptions to *Popular Mechanics, Vibe,* or *Soldier of Fortune* is soliciting business from you. He's probably irritating unless you like to listen to hip-hop while you and your Devil Dog buddies decide whether charcoal or propane might make a better backyard grill, but he's not necessarily doing anything illegal. On the other hand, if someone catches an ambulance-chasing lawyer passing business cards around an emergency room, that's legal solicitation (that's not to say allowed-by-law solicitation, but a still-illegal form of solicitation of the lawyerly variety), and it can land my colleagues in a big world of ethical excrement.

Soliciting a prostitute is something else entirely. Sincerely, Captain Obvious.

Now, *solicitation* in our situation means, on its most basic level, that someone has tried to engage someone else to do something criminal. That can fit more than just prostitution. Asking good old Clancy from the hardware store to murder your neighbor with a weedwacker is solicitation of murder, a serious felony. Smooth-talking your girlfriend's stepcousin into selling you a bag of weed is also solicitation.

But so is requesting a sex worker whose nom de plume is also an inventive Oreo flavor to let you perform the Angry Dragon—for a reasonable extra fee, of course. It doesn't even have to be that colorful. Requesting any sort of skin-to-skin shenanigans, even encoded, may end up saddling you with a solicitation charge, Don Juan.

I'm making it sound more straightforward than it usually is. A staggering number of clients facing a solicitation rap didn't solicit an actual sex worker at all.

WHEN YOU NEED AN ATTORNEY

They propositioned an officer posing as a nimble, long-legged beauty of the night named "Miss Kandy Mountain." Don't let cops fool you; those blue rascals are flexible—they can role-play on either the john's or the trick's side to nab their targets.

If you insist on paying for your jollies even though the powdered wigs have yet to loosen up about the regulations on this matter, then you'd better make sure that a roll of Magnums aren't the only prophylactic you've got in your pocket and read on . . .

BE ALLERGIC TO STINGS

You've probably heard from numerous sources that it's a bad idea to buy a night out knocking boots. It's not my business to tell you how to blend your protein shake, but we'll take that as a given.

What follows can go down more ways these days than ever, because we have the magic miracle machine that is the smart device. Cell, tablet, pager, berry, box, pad, pod, palm—the World Wide Web has a lot of big-kid playgrounds. Sure, there are still streetwalkers out there going old school, trading the information super-highway for actual streets, traversing afoot to offer potential customers a little curbside service. But there are also a slew of online avenues to erotic adventure and less-erotic jail time—or at least a fine.

The conventional way: guy's headed home, stressing, after a rough day at work. Bill in Accounting called him a scaredy-cat. Gayle in the mailroom lost his mail. He's a red-blooded American male and he would like to take the over/under on a $60 wager. A perfectly logical progression.

Most of us, if we've lived in any city for a reasonable amount of time, know the dark spots. Often the mean streets are all kinds of mean, but I'd guess based on experience that sometimes that's part of the appeal. The danger, you see.

So Mr. Old-Fashioned heads to a pool of light on a dark street corner where a lone streetwalker waits. She strolls up to his window and they chat. Maybe $50 for a handy-j with a rail-splitter or $100 for an around the world on a tramp steamer bound for Tokyo. I'm making these up—if they're real sex acts don't tell me what they really are—I'd like to preserve my innocence (okay, you got me, imagination).

As soon as that money passes from car to glitter-manicured hand, the woman steps back and the next thing you know it's an uncomfortable bracelet and a bus ticket for the big house, my friend. Your dance card is as full as the chow line, and Butch doing fifteen for aggravated assault has a reservation to ride that steamer with you all the way around the world. A hearty lesson learned: you suck at soliciting prostitutes.

NEW SCHOOL

Let's pause before we get to strategies, to learning how to be allergic to stings, and talk about the thoroughly modern man's way of seeking paid companionship: online ads.

I don't really know why folks aren't automatically suspicious of all online solicitation ads. They kind of follow a template: improbably attractive photograph of a male or female model (depending on which flavor you seek—clients certainly get snagged for seeking both, though cops will still tend to target guys seeking female companionship), with a come-hither message. Something like, "Hey, big man, I know exactly what you want and need and I'm ready to give that exact thing to you," followed by contact information. Don't call that number. This is the same shit Santa pulled, and the outcome is gonna be even more traumatic than that unanswered letter you sent to the North Pole in 1989 begging for that Pac-Man watch and a new skateboard for Michelangelo because the Teenage Mutant Ninja Turtles were your real prophets.

Why stuff your childhood trauma inside and focus

on the solicitation scenario? Because in a sting, there's a good chance cops are recording that phone call. They will use that to build the beginning of a case against you. If you discuss costs, specific kinds of frolicking, and when and where to meet up, all those juicy tidbits will be on record before you ever even walk out the door.

Cops set this stuff up nicely, and they aren't stupid. They'll usually pick a motel or low-priced hotel. It'll be a medium-cost place, one of the budget chains, usually. They'll rent a set of rooms, one for stationing personnel and monitoring the meeting room, where the solicitor will eventually appear in vivid color on video.

The undercover officer responsible for all the flirty talk on the phone will be wearing a wire. There will be a subtle script in play, one with which clients too often play a key role. Once the mark—let's say that's you in this case—is in place, the script for the encounter that began online plays out a lot like the old-timey street encounter.

- The undercover officer will make sure she's talking to the same person who made the "appointment."
- The undercover officer will try their best to ensure you two are there to trade pillow talk for dollars. Legally, for the police, this part can be pretty important.
- If the covert sex operative manages to establish the

bare bones facts before you even reach the room, the other officers on scene will swoop in to nab you. Unless you have a humiliation fetish, this is when the evening will stop being remotely arousing.

Here's the kicker: even if you arrive and your Spidey sense activates before you enter the building—which happens to plenty of guys—you may still get arrested! The police want that score, so they just might stretch charges into the fairly easily prosecuted "act in further-ance" of prostitution, which is the crime of simply *agreeing* to engage in sex-for-pay, whether or not you ever show up to do the deed.

GETTING OUT OF THE TRAP

You've been stung. Is it going to swell a little or will you blow up like one of those weird, spiny fish that inflate to four times normal size to scare off predators? Now it's time for strategies. Let me be your EpiPen.

First let's talk intentions. To prosecute a solicitation case, the prosecutor has to prove beyond a shadow of a doubt that you really wanted to launch your rocks and were willing to shell out for it. They need to prove that you intended to make the fabled beast with two backs.

This can make or break a case. Here's what the cops would like:

YOU: Yes, I would like to have you perform fellatio on my little Elvis. I will pay your best rate for this activity.

OFFICER: Certainly, sir. Money before services, please.

Of course, no one talks like that. Cops, for one thing, can't be too overt or they walk right into entrapment. So verbal games ensue:

YOU: Um, I was wondering—

OFFICER: Looking for company?

YOU: Yes, some company. With benefits.

Or something to this effect. If you are going to try to secure the services of a prostitute, be as vague as you can possibly manage. Not that I'm encouraging you to break any vice laws where you live, in any way. I'm just saying you should keep things unspecific, especially if you pride yourself on being a pretty straight-talking kind of guy. In this instance, frank clarity is your worst enemy. That first contact point, whether it's over e-mail, phone, or in person, can result in the exchange that sets up your defense later, if it turns out you fell for the long sting of the law.

A trickier defense that might be much more viable if you're the old-fashioned, chat 'em up on the street kind of dude—"Honestly, officer, I just saw an attractive woman and really wanted to get to know her better."

It might feel kind of forced, but awkward as a random street approach of some single woman alone at night may seem, the right attorney could sit you down and even convince you that's all you were seeking all along: a new friend. The defense is it didn't even occur to you that money might be involved. Again, just as in the "vague" defense, this is a time for a guy to make like he's perhaps not all that bright. The smart move is to play dumb.

Look, as long as you aren't one of those pig fuckers who knowingly solicits sex with someone who's underage, here's the good news: it's usually a misdemeanor. Soliciting a murder is definitely a felony, but soliciting a chance to grope the grapefruit with a consenting stranger for pay—class B or C, usually.

I say good news, but it's only good news if you are convicted of the crime. You don't have to accept that it's just going to go that way, because I sure don't.

Let me tell you about a few possible defenses an attorney might pull out of his or her hat to defend an accused patron of the curbside circuit.

- **The "there's no way this is actually a crime" defense.**
  It states it just isn't legally feasible to say you

SIDEBAR

Here's the frustrating deal about solicitation: from the defendant's perspective it can be hard to understand exactly why this is illegal. Seriously, you only *talked* about getting it on for the price of a large pancake house meal for two, but you didn't even get to sniff the syrup. You could, if you wanted to play paranoid conspiracy theorist for a moment, almost think of this kind of thing as a thought crime.

You thought about it, kind of talked about it, but you certainly didn't *do* anything.

Yeah, it's a bitch, but sometimes a crime can be half-baked and the law still calls it fully done. There are three main kinds of these lukewarm, semi-crimes: a crime of conspiracy, attempted crime, and—that's right—solicitation. Any of the three can really deflate your swaggering soufflé into a slice of humble pie.

Infuriating as it may be, the fact that conspiracy and criminal attempts are under the half-crime umbrella should explain why solicitation is there as well. If a political figure is assassinated and one guy pulled the trigger, but he did it after talking about how it would go down at length with two others and they egged him on and gave him ideas on how to do it—well, it's pretty easy to see how they would get taken in by investigators, too, right? Scheduling a date in your day planner with a prostitute is both a bit of an attempted crime and a crime of solicitation. You tried, after all, and didn't get that sweet cigar! And in trying, the law sees what you did as *soliciting* the person you wanted to pay for sex to break the law as well. You had a specific intention of doing that thing.

committed a crime. This is merely an okay solution, for my money. Well, your money. In a prostitution case it might be tough to prove. I mean, attorneys have to say stuff all the time that looks kind of ridiculous to the casual observer, but here, especially if you set the meeting up online, it'd be tough for me to keep a straight face when telling the court, "My client did nothing wrong, he set up that meeting in an anonymous no-tell motel with a sexy-sounding stranger to play a round of gin rummy." This is an approach to try with some other forms of solicitation, I guess, but it could seem pretty weak here.

- **If you make it in the door before getting busted, you could try the "Look, I totally stopped before it happened" defense.** It says you abandoned the effort. It's the sort of defense that might work if you were conspiring to commit a crime, then tipped the cops to bust the other conspirators. It's bad here because it implies you intended to do the booty boogie for the agreed-upon song fee, but said, "whooooaaa, partner" when the music started. It'd be hard to make that defense stack up, though I wouldn't be opposed to trying. And don't always take my word for it, there are as many perspectives on valid defenses out there as there are attorneys. I just wouldn't give it a go unless I thought I had a slam-dunk case of police forcing the issue, true entrapment.

- **"Man, I didn't even know this was a crime!"** There might be something to this one. And the cool thing is, especially in the case of online or phone contact with the undercover officer prior to the arrest, the cops might have given you the defense themselves. That's because when the vice meatballs post their ads, they avoid obvious wording like, "Totally looking to sex up a lonely man for money, let me make your penis happy." They have to use suggestive hints and euphemisms. How this defense could work: it's dirt common for prostitution to be disguised, in all sorts of settings, as "massage" services. It's the kind of thing most of us wink at each other about, sure. "Oh, yeah, 'deep massage,' I get it."

But that doesn't mean there isn't still one guy out there who might see an ad on a website or something and say, "Golly, I sure am tense! I could use a nice Swedish!"

That guy could be you. And then your defense is straightforward. "Your honor, I was just as shocked as anyone that the arresting officers believed I wanted my penis massaged. I have tight hamstrings!"

Summation

As with so many of the topics we're blazing through, there are aspects of this one I haven't even come close to addressing. There's the whole entrapment issue, for example. This is a common defense against a prostitution arrest, and it's usually valid. But vice squads get major coaching in how to avoid any appearance of having lured you into their loving embrace. Still, entrapment can happen, so if you're ever unfortunate enough to be in this situation remember to run through the experience in detail with your attorney, who will certainly know all the telltale signs of you having been suckered into a jam.

Let's imagine that in spite of being aware of the risks inherent in this kind of thing, your inner thrill seeker still pushes you to ring up your local Heidi Fleiss. Hopefully you have a better idea of what to say and do to keep the cops from taking your booty call and handing your ass right back to you.

The best advice is: don't do it. The Internet is just raring to delight your senses with all sorts of debauchery, and adult bookstores are stocked to the ceiling with artificial tools to help bring you real gratification. There are much better ways to get your name in the local newspaper.

Invitation to Not Murder

Like discovering a tube of pineapple-flavored lubricant next to a copy of the 1985 NBA Guide in your grandfather's bedside table, murder is a bell that you can't unring. Don't do it.

The end.

Well, it's the end of your life outside the stone house, anyway. So far we've been tripping the light fantastic, for the most part, talking about legal issues that seem downright fluffy compared to this one. But I didn't become a lawyer to avoid the heavy lifting. Hand me the barbells, because we're about to get weighty.

So . . . murder. Homicide.

Did you know those are two different things? They are. What's homicide? It's basically one person causing another person's death. It isn't always a criminal act. Homicide comes in many flavors. Intentional manslaughter: killing someone on purpose, perhaps because you were provoked into doing it. Unintentional manslaughter: accidentally running someone down with a vehicle, which is—you guessed it—vehicular manslaughter, for instance.

There are what's known as affirmative defenses to some homicides, too. Being insane at the time is one. Not insane in the eyes of the medical community necessarily, but legally insane, usually under the good old M'Naghten Rule, which asks if the killer knew that what they were doing was wrong when they did it. Another affirmative defense, of course, is being able to prove you acted in self-defense.

How is murder different?

Oh, man, let me count the ways. I'll try to avoid making your eyes cross, but it's worth digging into it a little bit just so you have a relatively clear idea as to what you might be up against if somehow you ever find yourself on the receiving end of a murder charge. Which, let's not pussyfoot around, would be a seriously shitty place to be. We're talking flash flood at the KOA, spontaneous slab avalanche on Everest, super-typhoon in Margaritaville.

First thing's first: murder is *also* homicide, yes. Next, one of my old refrains about the vagaries of the American legal system: wherever you live, what constitutes the act of murder will be a little different, according to the law. States have various degrees of murder charges available for purchase.

Old-fashioned common law—which is kind of like an oral history of judges' decisions going way, way back to the English way—framed up the varieties of murder pretty well. In common law, homicide becomes *murder* when the magic spell-like phrase "malice aforethought" enters the picture. If someone cuts you off on the highway and you think, "I'm going to kill that guy with my bare hands," then pull him over and do it, you had malice aforethought. It's deciding to do something you know is totally illegal, with no just cause. And no, "road rage" rarely works as a valid insanity defense.

Current, modern law breaks down the varieties of murder with malice aforethought something like this:

- **Taking a life on purpose, and having clear knowledge as to what you've done.** A planned, purposeful homicide equals first-degree murder. Some states even dub this "malice murder" just so it's clear that first degree equals "malice aforethought." A tangled lasso indeed.

- **Killing from reckless intent.** If a cowgirl riding through town wildly shooting her Colt Single Action in all directions accidentally breaks a heart with one of her bullets, that little lady was behaving recklessly. Common law quaintly called this "depraved-heart" murder. Murder in the second degree can fall under this heading, because reckless intent doesn't equal premeditated, planned homicide.

- **Especially heinous murder.** Poisoning, setting someone on fire, pretty much anything that involves killing-by-torture. Murders committed with unusual nastiness. Really vicious crimes like this are usually first-degree murder, though if you kept your victim alive for a bit so that they could watch you dine on their gallbladder, your attorney may want to consider having you plead that tricky insanity defense.

- **Felony murder.** That may seem redundant, but this subcategory is about murders that happen while the killer is committing another crime. Robber kills a guard while ripping off a bank? Felony murder. Sometimes you don't even have to pull the trigger in a situation like that. Some states have laws that say that if there are two robbers fleecing a joint, but only one pulls the trigger that offs a guard, the other robber can be held liable.

We're not hiking too far into the weeds. If you find yourself accused of killing with malice aforethought, my goal is pretty simple, even though murder itself isn't always all that straightforward. You are the Triangle Shirtwaist Factory, and this charge is the spark, the smoke, and every locked stairwell on the way down. If you follow these instructions closely, we might be able to wedge open a window for you.

SING ALONG WITH ME NOW

Shut up. Lips zipped. *¡Cállate!* Don't say a word. Yes, that's a pretty common refrain. Sing it in the shower like your favorite Britney Spears song. If you just can't bring yourself to heed that advice regarding a prostitution rap, or a drug charge, or whatever other misadventure you can dream up, listen now. The moment there's a dead body to be examined and an officer of the law in your face asking questions, shut up.

I know, I know, the impulse in this case, more than about anywhere else, will be to assume that by invoking your right to an attorney you must be somehow guilty. Cops rely on this, big time. They know it's a perfectly reasonable human instinct. And it is! But sometimes your gut is wrong. Give your attorney a call!

Anyway, take comfort, not many people get gored by the horns of a homicide allegation. It's unlikely you'll ever need to deal with all this rigmarole. But it's worth me repeating a point here, because it doesn't get more serious than homicide, and most of the time people accused of it, innocent or not, suck at dealing with the traumatic accusation. Silence, in this instance, is the first step in your imaginary folder marked "Contingency

Plan for Murder Charges I'll Probably Never Face, But Let's Be Safe, Just in Case." Or something a little punchier than that.

So: keep quiet and call your lawyer. If you take those two steps as gospel, then coping with the first steps of a murder allegation is pretty simple. As an innocent, wrongly accused party, your main enemy will be the impulse to protest.

The sworn peace officers with a solemn duty to get murderers off the street as soon as humanly possible really want you to speak freely and lawyerlessly. They would love to hear you object to your little heart's content. Cops—particularly those who've risen to detective—are masters of interrogation and selective interpreters of the answers they receive. And it is a no-win for you to engage this way, trust me on that. Why? Because even an innocent person will end up telling the same story in different ways. Especially if that innocent person is completely flustered by the idea that they might be a murder suspect. The understanding, compassionate officer on the other side of the interrogation table will interpret this as evidence of guilt and throw your ass in a holding cell quicker than the Zodiac Killer could lick a stamp.

So *shhhh*. And get a lawyer. Or gladly accept whomever the judge appoints for you. Now is the worst time imaginable to consider pro se.

OH, NO, OH, NO, IT'S OFF TO JAIL YOU GO

A lot of what we've been discussing prior to wading into the murder pond didn't necessarily involve actually ending up behind bars. Many charges that demand you get legal representation can come with an affordable bail. This sure as hell can change once murder enters the picture.

If the charge is murder in the first, bail will be too high to manage for all but the heirs and heiresses. And sometimes a judge won't even set bail, just to make sure you stay inside. The state believes you thought about it, maybe even planned it out, meant to do it, and to the state, that makes you a seriously dangerous dawg.

If you're innocently enjoying Panda Express with your grandma and a mall rat won't stop disrespecting sweet Nana until you toss that mouthy punk off the food court balcony and right into a pretzel fryer, that doesn't mean you can skip off to the gumball machine with your quarters; you're gonna need every penny. For a second-degree murder—usually thought to be an unplanned, spontaneous homicide—there will still be a pretty high bail. Same for a felony murder. Say you're a simple, humble car thief, but you run someone over as you make your getaway? That's felony murder, and you might as well be driving that pimped-out Porsche straight to Sing Sing.

I think you get the picture now. It does change a bit

if the charge is manslaughter, where the level of perceived negligence becomes a factor. A drunk driver killing a pedestrian certainly had no intention of killing anyone, but being drunk at the wheel was one crime, and it involved seriously negligent behavior. Chances are the bail will be high, but possibly doable if, again, you've got even semi-deep pockets. And this isn't like the, "Oh, oopsie daisy," of breaking Pop-Pop's antique cookie jar—you'd better be ready to prove to the court with words and tears (and more) that your drunk ass is legitimately sorry.

LIPS SEALED, LAWYERED UP, WHAT NOW?

I've got my biggest, widest brush out now, since until you're actually faced with a murder case, specifics might be meaningless.

Let's start with obtaining your lawyer. You might start with a legal aid attorney if you are financially challenged or even middle class. While these guys and gals might be pure gold when arguing to get you out of a solicitation charge, murder is a big level up, and in many jurisdictions, the pay for either case is going to be the same. So legal aid is a gamble.

Assuming you've hired a lawyer, I'll address a practical aspect: money. You don't need the Oracle to tell you that with a murder charge of any kind—malice, manslaughter, felony, whatever—getting a good attorney suddenly becomes a more crucial investment than that IRA you've been working on since undergrad.

The good counselors aren't necessarily affordable. Then again, if they think the case is winnable, and, double bonus, if the case is also notable, they may work with you at least in how they'll accept payment. Most firms bill for hours, but it's not unreasonable to ask for a ballpark figure, a lump-sum fee. A case with simple elements that seems like a pretty sure win may not cause a financial apocalypse for the accused. Complicated cases full of tricky forensic evidence are something else again.

WHAT IF THE GLOVES SLIPPED OFF IN THE RUCKUS?

We fight murder charges like our hair's on fire, man. Like our hair is on fire but it hasn't melted our brains. No weaklings here. If you are asking for brass tacks, okay—here are typical defenses we may select from our quiver of legal arrows.

We're safe in our attorney-client cocoon now, and I'll present some possible defenses to use against any murder charge—defenses other than "not guilty." Contingency plans have to include preparing for the worst.

SIDEBAR

I know you're thinking this chapter will never apply to you, but you may find yourself like many of your fellow churchgoing, baseball-loving, apple-pie-eating, red-white-and-blue-blooded American citizens: surprised to find yourself at the bum end of a murder charge. Or close, like an attempted murder charge.

Let me tell you about Claus. You've probably heard of Claus. Claus von Bülow. Or maybe not, this was a while back.

Claus was a wealthy man, married to Sunny, an heiress. One day in 1982, our pal Claus found himself on the hook for what police said was an attempt to end Sunny's life via insulin overdose. The diabetic socialite didn't die, but remained in a coma the rest of her life.

Claus had money out the gazoo. It oozed from the man. That the couple were named Claus and Sunny and lived in a historic home in the opulent hamlet of Newport, Rhode Island, should be enough to emphasize the level of swanktown involved here.

So Claus could, admittedly, throw one hell of a healthy legal defense team at the attempted murder charge against him. He did, and he lost. He was sentenced to thirty years in prison.

Appeals followed, handled by legendary defense attorneys who tracked down every expert in every field relevant to the defense's case and threw them at the court. It took a few years but Claus's conviction was finally

(continued)

reversed; at a second trial, he was found not guilty. Sunny, it seemed, had succumbed to misadventures with various chemical cocktails that never should have been found in her bloodstream. But the von Bülow trials took up a lot of room in the news in the mid-eighties, and in spite of being cleared, Claus's name became almost synonymous with creepy, potentially murderous rich guys, in a pop culture sort of way.

What I'm getting at here is the odds are good you don't have the screw-you level of fat stacks to throw around that Claus did. And he was, after all, found guilty the first time around. So if Claus jumped off a bridge, maybe you should just wave and bid him farewell . . . then get the hell out of there before anyone shows up asking questions.

Or in the case of being put on trial for murder, the worst possible worst.

- **The crazies.** I know "crazy" is an insensitive term. Murder is an insensitive act, to say the least. If the prosecution has something like a slam dunk, though, we've got to consider the possibility you were dealing with "diminished capacity" when everything went down. An attorney will ask if you've ever seen a psychiatrist or psychologist; if you've ever been on psychiatric meds for depression, bipolar disorder, schizophrenia. Hell, for

ADHD. If we hang our hat on a mental disorder defense, we'll have to put it in writing. We'll have to offer proof your *cabeza*'s a broken bell tower and the bats are flying circles. Drawbacks to this line of fire are many. There's the M'Naghten Rule, which I mentioned earlier, and its cousin, the newer Irresistible Impulse Test. These damned things are so narrow, so nineteenth century, that they don't really allow for all that psych folks know these days about the way mental illness works on the brain. The worst part of this defense, depending on your perspective, is that you will end up confined anyway. Not guilty by reason of insanity is no "get out of jail free" card. It's a "don't go to jail, go to a mental hospital where there are potentially many more volatile and dangerous people freely roaming the halls with you" card.

- **A related defense, again one to be used when the prosecution's got what looks like all the goods: substance-related impairment.** Or just impairment with some physical basis, like a head injury. If an attorney can prove a murder was committed because the killer had injury-related brain damage in the part of your gray matter that prevents you from homicidal behavior, this can lead to acquittals or at the very least, a lower-level charge with less severe penalties.

- **There's also "heat of passion."** It's the defense of choice for wronged husbands and wives everywhere—folks whose semi-rational response to finding a loved one bumping uglies with an unapproved partner is white-hot, murderous rage. Do not pass go; this one is going to end in jail time anyway.

There's a wily thing worth mentioning here called an Alford plea. It's a special animal, a zebra in a stampede of horses named "guilty" and "not guilty." The Alford is a guilty plea, but when you make it, you're not admitting guilt. It says, "I didn't do it, but you've got a case that sure makes it look like I did."

Don't confuse Alford with pleading "no contest"—aka "nolo contendere." Our little buddy nolo is not any kind of a guilty plea, and it's a pretty special case. I don't think courts even accept a nolo plea in some states, because it gets in the way of the three-strikes laws—legislation that dings you with hefty penalties, up to life in prison, if you are convicted of three felonies. An Alford plea can count toward those strikes and a jury can be informed if you get in trouble again in the future. Nolo contendere cannot. However, a court doesn't even have to accept nolo. So now you know, they aren't interchangeable.

And the Alford plea? It usually still gets you plenty of jail time, but you may be able to strike a better deal than you would get if you threw yourself on the mercy of the court—plus, you get to maintain your innocence. I'm sure that'll keep you warm on those cold, cinder-block nights.

Summation

Defenses against a murder charge can boil down to two basic categories: not guilty, didn't do it, and "yeah, I did it, but you still can't blame me for it."

The American justice system is hard-coded with the idea that we're all innocent until proven guilty. It's basic, been with us from the beginning.

But in reality, the moment investigators settle on you as a murder suspect, that old presumption might as well be Bigfoot.

Let's say you didn't do it. Hell, let's assume you didn't! The first thing you and your attorney will want to find is an alibi. Solid alibi, easily proven? Good as gold. Shaky alibi, say, hard to verify and delivered by a very sympathetic family member? Eh . . . not so much. That will provide some prosecutorial wiggle room, and they will whip out their Hula-Hoops and shimmy your story straight into the trash can.

Without an alibi—and too often, folks don't have an alibi good enough to fly—the case gets far more complex. "Reasonable doubt" becomes your best friend, your Bible, your inspirational poster of a cat clinging to a tree branch. It's only earned with very hard work by you and your attorney—and slack work from the other side—that you build that doubt in the judge's or the jury's mind.

We're all innocent until proven guilty, yes. But I'd still be sleeping on a futon in the back of a nail salon with off-limits cucumber water if everyone stayed innocent and never needed to fight to prove it. If it comes down to battle, call your Saul and soldier forth.

PART III

Good Ways to Not Make Things Worse

Avoiding Jail

One thing about jail, about most penal facilities: the wardrobe options are as bountiful as cool springs in the Sahara. I mean, seriously, who looks good in an orange jumpsuit with matching orange slippers? *No one.* Okay, I knew a guy back in Illinois who wore it well, and he did become governor, eventually. But see, four Illinois governors have gone to jail in the last thirtysomething years, so that one guy doesn't really prove anything.

I'm including ideas on how to avoid jail here, but we should also talk about how to skirt mandatory sentencing laws. Sometimes you need a life coach, and I'm here to give you a pep talk and blow the whistle if you start swimming out of your existential lane.

To be clear: I'm not trying to condemn anyone or criticize the lives they've led so far. Clients rely on their defense attorneys not to do that! I'm talking about practical shit when all is said and done. Strategies, tactics, plans. You don't have to be MacGyver using a paper clip to defuse a bomb strapped to the bottom of a boat to be a superb tactician. With the right tools, we can take a little bit of leverage and nudge your explosive life back into calm waters.

The Friends You Keep

Let's talk about your friends. Not just me. I'm talking about Suzy, who you've known since third grade, and who—despite her slightly caustic personality—you swear wouldn't ever hurt a fly or persuade you to hot-wire a car . . . again. Sometimes, when I first meet a client, they've already been through a round or two of trouble. They have an idea of what the whole incarceration thing is like. We cross paths because they're poised to repeat a grade at the Fresh Meat Finishing School.

Most of the time, this déjà-vu has come about because

once they repaid their debt to society, they went right back to running with the same troublemaking friends that helped get them into hot water in the first place.

I can't tell you what to do and be sure you'll do it. I wish attorneys had that kind of sway over clients—we'd all be the Atticus Finches or Perry Masons we set out to be. But it's your life and your choices, no matter how wild the ride gets. Here's a thought: maybe some of your friends are part of the bad choices that led to you being popped in the first place. That one friend who brings out the "best" in you might actually be the one who seduces you over to the Dark Side.

So here's a point to consider: if it feels disloyal to end a potentially toxic relationship altogether, at least consider pumping the brakes with your criminal soul mate. Definitely try to stay away if you've currently got a case in court; the judge will view it as an act of good faith. And one act of good faith can be the difference between showering in the luxury of your own home and bartering unfavorable favors with Krazy-Eyed Kevin for a bar of Dial in Cellblock D.

It isn't that your friends don't care about you. You certainly give a damn about them! But sometimes the best path really can be the straight and narrow one. There's nothing wrong with working a solid job with a health plan and a reliable nine-to-five schedule. Sure, that gig might not pay as well as whatever business you were in before, but honest work, in the eyes of the court, is much better than no work at all. Plus: boring jobs have perks, too! You might find wholesale prices on electronics are just as sweet as wholesale prices on street candy.

I know this might be asking something that feels impossible. I mean, life falls into a groove, you know? We get comfortable with making money a certain way, with the acquaintances we have. These are the pals that hid you in the bed of their pickup truck after you got caught skinny-dipping in your trigger-happy neighbor's pool—how can you turn your back on true amigos like that? But, a good friend will understand when you are trying to make something out of yourself. They'll be proud of you. Which means that maybe once things settle, you can go back, get together, and laugh about the fun you crazy kids had in the good old days.

If you're not getting a tan from the sunshine just blazing out of my ass, then I'll put it another way: if a client is a regular visitor to the county facilities, just waiting for a permanent spot up in the state penitentiary, it's because one or more of their relationships is taking a sledgehammer to their well-intentioned knees and hobbling them out of the good life they deserve.

If your best buddy is a drug dealer and you know it and are down with that, he or she may get caught and you could go down with them. You want to play shuffleboard in the shadow of a volcano? Don't be surprised when it all blows up and your bungalow gets a lava shellacking.

So: work with what you've got in order to show acts of good faith to the court. If you have decent family and have been disconnected from them, reconnect. If someone will give you a legit job, the kind that takes all those wonderful taxes out of your machine-printed paycheck, take the damned thing with a smile—no matter how unappealing it may seem. Shit, shave every day. Set alarms and get up when they go off. Jog for five minutes every morning. Make it work.

Attorneys depend on having clients, and criminal defense lawyers specifically need, well, criminals. There will always be plenty of the latter to go around. Some made an escalating series of bad choices, and now aren't able to extricate themselves from the criminal life. Some may even have discovered that they liked it. That's fine! People get their thrills in different ways. But, once in a while, an attorney comes across someone who still has some choices left to make. That might be you. And those choices don't have to be shitty ones.

Why Avoid Jail?

It's in both our best interests for you to stay out of jail, but if you wind up on the inside, it helps to be prepared. Forewarned, forearmed. So let's talk about what's going on in there that you might not know about. I'm no expert, but I've certainly known a few who were, and—surprise! I've learned that it's both not quite as bad as you might imagine and much, much worse than you've heard. This isn't me shaking manacles in your face, barking commands in some *Scared Straight* scenario; this is an attempt to make my job and your life a little easier.

Don't Worry So Much About Your Ass

If there's one thing that everyone seems to know about prison, it's that if you're new, you might as well be the last showgirl on the *Titanic* for the amount of lap-dance requests you are about to receive—some more forceful than others. And while you may still be nursing resentment that you weren't ever crowned Prom King or Queen, I've got some good news: you may not be any more popular in lockup than you were in high school. The fact is, particularly for the anxious male client, there may be worse things to worry about behind bars than nonconsensual guy-on-guy action.

Yes, it does happen. There are *Deliverance*-style rednecks and other sexually motivated psychos galore behind bars, no doubt about it, and they've been known to turn other prisoners into their cinder-block concubines. There are coalitions on the outside dedicated to fighting this aspect of prison life, and bless 'em, I hope they win the battle.

But the truth is, it's not a given that it will happen to you. Or that it will ever happen, until you're in the mood to try something new with a consenting partner. This might be the rare comfort I can offer: if you're a freshman in adult detention, you might want to worry less about being sexually victimized and more about getting beaten up, killed outright, or falling in with a group on the inside who make your rough crowd on the outside look like a bunch of Presbyterian preschoolers. No one wants to go in for a ninety-day stretch (brilliantly negotiated down from a few years by your well-dressed and golden-tongued attorney), only to have a drug possession charge turn ninety days into thirty-six months. Why would you do that to your hardworking and accomplished legal counsel?

Most of the time, just about everyone behind bars is simply trying to survive until they see the sunlight again. They're trying to do that with as little fuss as possible so they can get back to doing mattress push-ups with the assenting ass of their choice. Some of the things that can cause fuss follow.

Phone Privileges

Phone use is a big deal when legally you are only allowed to use whatever the facility makes available. Of course prisoners can get cell phones smuggled in, but who wants to use a flip phone that's been marinating in Jerry's sweetest-smelling orifice? Also, getting caught using one is only going to add time to your sentence, since they are considered contraband pretty much everywhere, much like drugs or alcohol.

Individual protocols vary from state to state and facility to facility, but prisoners who need those phones to touch base with family (or their charming and concerned legal counsel) tell me a few basic principles govern prison phone use. It's good for your neck if you know this beforehand, and good for my karma to help a neck or two:

- **Using the phone is a privilege in lockup.** No real constitutional protections apply, unless you need to call your attorney. It can be snatched away faster than a belly-button ring in an MRI machine if you don't play nice.

- **Some places require inmates to submit a list of people they're most likely to call.** That means Mom, Dad, Uncle Ernie, Auntie Jim, Bob your pastor. Maybe don't include the last ten guys who (allegedly) purchased hydrocodone from you.

- **Many facilities limit phone time.** You might get a mere fifteen minutes to make a collect call. Talk fast and plan ahead.

- **If you're lucky, you may end up someplace where phone use isn't time restricted.** At least, not officially—it will still be time restricted in practice, because that phone is a big-ass deal to *everyone,* and if you hog it, truckloads of woe unto you. There are shanks being made from layers of hardened paper just waiting to get stuck in the kidneys of an inmate who's gabbing the night away like a teenager whose parents let her install a private line in her bedroom.

- **Your conversation can be monitored.** Assume it will be monitored. Talk accordingly, and don't assume they won't spot a coded conversation. If you want to go that route, work out the code before you need it, and make sure it's specific to you and the person with whom you'll need it—who may even be your attorney, you never know. I may be a fairly well-rounded Renaissance man, but even I will need a weekend to brush up on my Navajo before we unleash the Marines on Iwo Jima, *capisce?*

We haven't even touched on the booming prison phone call racket. Forget dimes—folks are sometimes charged as much as $14 a *minute* just for the privilege of talking to an incarcerated loved one. The Federal Communications Commission has been working to change that, but it gives you some idea of just how bad it sucks for people's bank accounts to simply check up on their mom's health or their kids' grades once they're behind bars.

All this to say: you have to be careful and respectful when sharing that phone with two hundred other people who are all some level of pissed-off that they're biding time in the slammer. Another reason to avoid incarceration, then—no one wants to get stabbed or their jaw broken over five minutes on a phone that already smells like the last guy's morning slug of toilet wine.

Personal Space

Cells are cramped, bare spaces purposefully devoid of light and life. Begonias don't even like them, and they're suckers for dark, cozy spots. True, many minimum security facilities have more open plans now, which come with their own problems, but no matter where you land, you and the rest of the local convicts are stuck in a box together. There is no leeway for bad roommates. Forget college, where that might have gotten you a passive-aggressive Post-it note pasted to your mirror—now it could get you killed.

Here are a few suggestions of how to avoid pissing off your bunkmate:

- **Being messy is an easy way to get in trouble with your assigned cohabitant.** Think about your personal habits. A charming desire to conserve water by not flushing at home can become a shank of contention between you and a psychopath nicknamed Mickey Everest in your prison cell.
- **Not paying much attention to who owns what stuff is a dangerous dalliance.** I'm not even talking stealing another inmate's property, which is a whole other level of risky business; I'm talking about

using the wrong comb. Sure, you and your girl-friend might be lackadaisical about handing that big brush back and forth in the comfort of your own rent-by-the-week motel, but the Belo Brigada gang member occupying the top bunk while awaiting trial for assault with a deadly weapon might have a different idea about sharing personal property.

- **Casual everyday rudeness like cutting in the sand-wich line doesn't often get more than nasty looks if you're at the Safeway.** On the inside, it can get you beaten into something that looks like a mixed-berry Jell-O salad. Prison can be tough on the pushy and ill-mannered; Mr. Everest and Señor Brigada can find a lot of common ground in agreeing that you're an asshole and you need to be disciplined.

I am not equipped to be cellblock six's own Emily Post, but hopefully these etiquette tips give you an idea of how to stay on the good side of the great minds behind the world's fastest nickname generator before someone dubs you "Cheezy Puffs" and takes away your toothbrush privileges.

The Guards Are Not Your Friends

In way too many correctional institutions, the people you most don't want to cross are the proud high school graduates wielding the Tasers and the clubs—your unfriendly neighborhood prison guards.

They are a uniformed minority doing a nasty job, doing their best to keep an orange-clad mass of pent-up muscle from rolling right over them and through the walls.

Fact is, though, they have the power to make their charges' lives miserable nine days a week.

- **Being friendly with the guards is a bad idea.** Other inmates peg you as a suck-up, and so do the guards. Worse than a suck-up—they might think you're a snitch. There are times when, in spite of the immovable "no snitching" code cemented in the foundation of almost any form of criminal community, snitching might be the right thing to do. No one in prison seems to agree with this, and even guards who see you this way might like you even less than they already do.
- **A good baseline rule for being incarcerated is to not trust a single person, and this goes for the guards as well.** Say a prayer to your preferred saint and throw those feel-good-isms you learned from the

nuns about trusting your neighbor out the window. Because here, your neighbor might want to shiv you. As hard as this revelation can be on the first-time innocent awaiting trial—someone accustomed to trusting authority—here, the authority sees you as just another chunk of wood in the Jenga stack.

- **In the metaphorical card game of prison life, don't play against guards.** They hold the ace of all aces: solitary confinement. They will slap it down like a Wild in a heated Uno stand-off, and you'll be irreversibly screwed and completely alone. Unless you're Dr. David Bowman (and, actually, he had HAL 9000 to keep him company), nothing good comes of complete isolation. Twenty-three hours a day in an itty-bitty room with just your own thoughts? No, thank you. I'm guessing you could fill a book of Mad Libs with more enjoyable forms of agony.

There Is No Graceful Way Out of This Now

The best way to keep choosing your own wardrobe on a daily basis is to have a winning defense strategy.

Every attorney is going to look for this first, above all else. We'll look for alibis, look for proof of innocence. We'll pick apart every piece of the prosecution's case we can. We want to see you walking freely into your bank of choice to pick up a cashier's check for our reasonable fees.

Due to cosmic imbalance or whatever causes shitty things to happen to good people, the things we want to happen don't always come to pass. Let's assume, hypothetically, that you get convicted. If the state mandates some kind of prison time, we'll fight to get the least amount possible at the least restrictive kind of facility. We want you to be rehabilitating comfortably in a cell that looks like a freshman dorm room, mini-fridge and all. You can take some horticulture classes, maybe drop a new album from the recording studio—we'll make your six months feel like a summer vacation in Ojai. Ideally.

But sometimes, you don't have to go to jail at all! If there isn't mandated time behind bars, we might explore some of the following:

- **Diversion.** We couldn't convince the jury you were fully innocent? The prosecution's case was too strong? I'm damn sure going to try another avenue, one called "Diversion Boulevard." This is most often a young person's penalty, or a first-time offender's. What happens is the case is *diverted* from the prosecution moving forward. It just stops at a certain point. However, diversion doesn't let anyone off the hook. You'd still be required to show some responsibility, under no less than the direct supervision of the police. Someone who gets into a diversion program might have to participate in one or more of the following:

- *School.* If the offender was arrested for some kind of drug crime, especially drug use, they might be put in an antidrug education program. The good folks who run the program hope it will illustrate where you went wrong and encourage you to never do it again. There are court-ordered classes for just about every misdemeanor-level crime you can imagine, and you can sometimes take them online through the power of Wi-Fi and Web cameras. So, this option isn't so bad—you grab a six-pack, put your copy of "Wild Things" on mute in the background, and learn about anger management from the comfort of your own La-Z-Boy.

- *Community Service.* This is a pretty common diversion and it's not bad. It feels so easy, you might be tempted to skip out on it—but you best follow through if you're committed to a life away from Brutalist architecture. Community service can offer a pleasantly wide variety of activities, from a breezy day spearing trash by the roadside to visiting schools in an effort to ensure the kids don't end up knee-deep in shit like you did. You'll get some vitamin D, work your quads, become your neighborhood's Dudley Do-Right—not too shabby!

- *Court-Ordered Abstention.* This is basically the court saying, "If you don't do this particular thing," (or) "If you avoid these people" for a specific period of time, you won't have to go to jail. Say your kid hacked into his school's grading software and gave himself a perfect four-point-oh. Instead of adding a jail sentence to the kid's tenuous future, a judge might order that the kid doesn't use computers with Internet connections unsupervised for the rest of his formative years.

- *Restitution*. Pay what you owe. If the thing that put you in court in the first place caused damages in any way, sometimes agreeing to restitution can keep you out of jail. Unfortunately, restitution often gets ordered along with jail time, too. If you are going to be required to pay it, you obviously want the no jail time restitution. Otherwise, you'll find yourself behind bars with barely enough money in your jail account to buy beanie-weenies, and you'll also owe a few thousand to whomever you wronged on the outside. Not to mention, you'll probably owe attorney fees and court costs.

- **Withheld adjudication.** This option is different from diversion. It's the court saying, "Let's see what you do to fix some stuff before we pass sentence." It isn't necessarily available for a lot of things, but when it is, it's a handy way to stay free to fight another day. Or to not fight, if that's why you were arrested, Rocky. Withheld adjudication is exactly what it sounds like: the court will agree to withhold judgment. Then, if you successfully complete probation, remain a fully upstanding citizen who demonstrates no further inclination to commit a crime, a conviction is never entered on your record. It's the closest you're going to get to time-travel.

These options may not seem like a bowl of fresh Michigan cherries to you, but they are infinitely more easy to swallow than the version of events that has you spotting reps for a convicted murderer named Bubba who outweighs you by two hundred pounds. Perspective, my friend.

Summation

There's only so much we attorneys can do to forewarn you about possible consequences and arm you with contingency plans. I'm not saying we want to see you behind bars or committing crimes—hell, if people stopped breaking laws, I'd practically be out of a job.

Know that whomever you've got in your corner, even if they're faced with a can't-win case on paper, they will do their goddamnedest to make it turn out the best for you. Even if your case lines up such that you're walking into a prearranged marriage between your ass and a guilty verdict, there are still plenty of ways to keep you free of incarceration.

Stop Snitching!
(Until You Learn How to Snitch)

Nobody likes a tattletale. We learned that way back when we snuck cigarettes on the playground. As the sage elders of yore often said: snitches get stitches.

I'm not encouraging anyone to risk a neck by declaring that it's necessary to rat on their co-conspirators. Popular vote says rats are malicious, they're working off a personal agenda, and there's nothing creepier than those beady red eyes.

But! There *are* times when turning rat and becoming an informant can actually be principled. Sometimes, it's the right thing to do.

So how do you know? Much like when you're trying to decide if it's time for a little more absorbency below deck, it depends. When you're dealing with legal issues, and especially with criminal law, it comes down to: what's in it for you? What's the moral balance, you know? Because sometimes, opening the lid on the toilet and luring passersby to witness the aftermath of an epic shit before the janitor makes the nightly rounds is your best possible course of action, in spite of how far outside your comfort zone it falls. It's a load off your mind, and maybe a load off your expected prison stay.

What if we were to drop the word "snitch" for a

moment and use another word—"whistle-blower?" Suddenly, it feels like a very different thing to do, doesn't it? A noble thing!

Is it? Well, a guy named Ralph Nader made the word "whistle-blower" mainstream back in the 1970s because "snitch" and "informer" had begun to sound unappealing. All that civil unrest going down in the late sixties was way too interesting to the FBI, so old J. Edgar Hoover sent his crew-cut boys to find hippies and activists who could be turned stool pigeon. Nader used "whistle-blower" to reclaim the righteousness of telling the truth about wrongdoing, so no one would confuse that type of informant with your run-of-the-mill street-corner snitch.

Now that we've cleared that distinction up, let's talk strategy.

Always Tell Your Attorney

An oldie but a goody. It may never be more important than when you've got the goods on someone or something—the "something" being some kind of organization. Because (and I know you knew I was going to mention it eventually) once we've established a paid relationship, we've got attorney-client privilege, and that is a beautiful, beautiful thing. As far as I'm concerned, that's the relationship all those sweet sonnets are about.

Whatever your snitching situation, whenever it occurs, if you know it's about legal wrongdoing, there's a grand old reason to run it up the flagpole and let an attorney see if it's going to flap in the breeze.

If it's me looking at what kind of truth you have to drop, I want to work out the best strategy for Team You, every time. The stone cold facts are these—if you have something to tell that is definitely going to work in your favor, and shift the spotlight away from your own misdeeds, well, my friend, let's pursue it. It's like spilling your martini on a bartender right before directing his attention toward a giant tidal wave about to crash into the bar—yeah, what you did wasn't cool, but he's got bigger and wetter things to worry about now.

So what does whistle-blowing look like? Perhaps you and me, side by side, sipping vinegar-flavored coffee in a cramped room that smells like stale pastries and fear while we paint a verbal picture of what it is that you might know for the police or whomever the investigating body is. The attorney's extremely important job here is to ensure that while you're spilling the beans, you don't do something that negates the goodwill that you're building up with the boys in blue, like revealing that you're complicit in another crime. Or that you have committed even more crimes than the cops were aware of in the first place. The point is: you might have a bargaining chip, so it's your best move to let your attorney size that chip up before you play it. As similar as they might look, there's a big difference between a $500 purple and a $1 blue. To keep you from getting screwed over, assume that your attorney is the only one in the room who isn't color-blind and trust their instincts before betting too big.

If you're in an interrogation room alone with an investigator, they might try and convince you it's cool to talk to them, a friendly face, just to get everything out in the open. That guy or gal will definitely be trying to wring something incriminating out of you, no matter how much you think you're buying yourself an invitation to the precinct's annual holiday party.

An important thing to keep in mind when your personal B-29 bomber is carrying an explosive piece of intel? It's possible the cops might already be in the know, especially if it involves a group of people. They'll probably string you along anyway. It's an investigative thing, and yes, they are totally allowed by law to do it.

So: rehearse with your attorney before you talk to anyone with a badge. "My roommate turned five people into hamburger macaroni for the bake sale and I said nothing because who wants to ruin a bake sale? Nobody!"

Share the recipe with your attorney first. "My cellmate is the block enforcer and he's having sex with all the guards who work third shift!" Let your attorney look through the peephole first. The same information a client is convinced is the hot ticket to save their ass—or at least get them a mattress pad with springs once they're on the inside—could wind up making their defense strategy useless. Tell your lawyer the whole truth and nothing but the truth so that he or she can keep you from using that truth to incriminate yourself.

Always Tell Your Attorney, Part 2: Whistle-Blower Boogaloo

All whistle-blowing is snitching, but not all snitching is whistle-blowing.

Maybe if there is a real difference between the way people look at snitching now and the way it was perceived back in those happy, high times, it's that "no snitching" has been kind of encoded into the criminal life, and it can feel singular, personal. There are some perfectly good reasons for that. Yes, it's a mistrust of the police that stops people from coming forward, but it's also a matter of self-preservation. Drop a dime on the guy you saw shoot up that bodega and you take one dude off the street, good for you—but if he's in a gang, there's a very real chance they won't just put you in their crosshairs, but your whole family.

But whistle-blowing . . . there is a reason there are firms that specialize in that. Even if it was supposed to be just a more pleasant word for snitching, it's taken on its own meaning. The right whistle-blower at the right time is a goddamned hero—and a hero is a dangerous thing to be.

I won't try to pull too much history professor shit on you, but: when a lot of people think whistle-blower now, they think of Karen Silkwood.

Karen was a humble technician working at a nuclear power plant.

She noticed that there was a lot of slack bullshit afoot at the plant, lapses in health and safety protocols that could end up killing people who worked there. She decided to gather up all the evidence she could and deliver it not to a lawyer, but to a reporter for *The New York Times*. A few miles out from her rendezvous, Karen's car left the road. It skidded a good distance before diving off an embankment. The packet she'd brought with her that was going to rip the lid off her employer's dangerous issues? Mysteriously gone from her car and never recovered.

Whatever caused Karen Silkwood's car crash, that

"mysterious force" probably didn't realize that her mission would end up making her a martyr not only to people who believe nuclear power is dangerous, but for people who want to call bullshit on nefarious organizations everywhere.

Silkwood-the-hero is an inspiration. Silkwood-the-deceased woman in an Oklahoma field is a cautionary tale. Cases like hers—and other famous cases, like the one that made Erin Brockovich a celebrity—have inspired some law firms to focus solely on representing folks who think there's an alarm that needs to be sounded, and they're the big red bell.

If you've got the goods on any kind of large organization or company—doesn't matter if they're privately owned or public—and you think you are exposing illegal, screwed-up actions, you're a classic whistle-blower à la Silkwood. The good news is, you have something available she didn't in the 1970s: law firms with the infrastructure to protect you.

That's not to say any attorney worth a damn can't handle a whistle-blower case. They can. But the bigger the organization you're up against, the more attorneys you'll probably need.

Example: you know for a fact that the crew of a local pawn shop moonlights building special novelty bongs for people addicted to anything they can turn into

SIDEBAR

I wanted to come back to the whole question of "snitch" versus "whistle-blower" one more time. It's easy to think of them as distinct at this point, right? Snitches are traitors of trust, and whistle-blowers are heroes going up against The Man, in all The Man's incarnations.

In all the talk everyone does about snitches being ass-holes among assholes in the criminal cosmos, it's impor-tant to note that even if a snitch is breaking a pinkie-swear with their blood brothers, they're doing it to take some-one pretty bad out of commission, often at great personal risk. My goal for clients never changes, and I'm sure this is true of criminal defense attorneys everywhere—if the bottom line is that the snitching is going to help you out of a jam, we have to take a cold, hard look at the choice. It's not something you should decide to do on a whim. Your lawyer should make sure you know what you might be getting into. They'll tell you if you've got a sweet bar-gaining chip or if you're asking for a hot date with the local hitman.

No good deed goes unpunished, so make sure you and your attorney survey the options before you go turning tricks for the state. Hopefully, you can absolve yourself of your sins and make the world a better place, but if the risks outweigh the reward—pause a beat to consider before running into the fray, Lancelot. You might bring down the kingdom to swat at a fly.

a vapor—and they also sell the soon-to-be-inhaled illegal goods themselves. If you report this one-stop shop, it's a whistle-blowing moment.

It's not the same kind of whistle-blowing moment, however, as learning a giant dog food manufacturer is intentionally selling meat-coated particle board to pet lovers nationwide to turn a higher profit margin. If you gather evidence of that, you probably *do* want to bring it to the attention of a specialized firm. Those guys will know that the Department of Labor has all kinds of rules in place to help protect whistle-blowers with a righteous cause.

Summation

There's a good reason some specialized law firms refer to their whistle-blowing cases as "complex cases." A whistle-blowing case can be like a Swiss egg, a Fabergé watch. It's delicate and time-consuming. Not to mention the fact that with whistle-blowers, it's all too often a David-and-Goliath situation, with a single person going up against an army in Armani. Guys with perfect hair and shiny teeth who are all too happy to keep the plaintiff's firm swamped in boxes of discovery from now till the end of days. Before you pucker up those heroic lips and put your lifeguard training to good use, take a quick look around to make sure you're prepared to agitate the sharks swimming just below the surface of the pond. Your lawyer will be able to measure the dangers, and let you know where and when it's time to blow.

It's Not *All* About the Benjamins, Baby, but They Sure Do Play an Important Role

Like all hardworking Americans, attorneys deserve to get paid. The common knock on us lawyers is that we get paid too much, or that we prosper off the misfortune of others. There are a few bad apples in every bushel, sure, but that doesn't take away all the benefits of a good apple in your lunch box. Most of us attorneys truly want to be good apples, looking out for your overall health. But meanwhile, we gotta make our lunch money, just like you.

Most attorneys know full well that no one will listen to us complaining about issues related to getting our paydays. Even other attorneys, unless we end up in the bizarre position of engaging one to pursue outstanding fees because we don't have time to handle our own cases and file suit for delinquents, too.

I know people hear "lawyer" and assume there's a fine European roadster parked out back. Not always. The average attorney makes a little over $100,000 a year, sure, but a ton of attorneys scrape by with much less, all while paying back massive law school debt.

I know what's up, though. Your fingers are playing me the tiniest violin. So I'll say, simply: pay your lawyer. Here are a few things about legal fees my fellow officers of the court might object to me putting out there, but as my prospective client, I want to make sure you're prepared for everything—including me:

The Mysterious, Secret World of Legal Fees

I'm not in the business of giving anyone else business if I don't have to, but if we can have a brief heart-to-heart here: most attorneys are doing the best job they can. Every day they're shuffling, shuffling—scheduled court appearances, documents to file, documents to examine, billing to render, one-on-ones with prosecutors or opposing counsel. . . . Come on, you see what I'm getting at. It's a job that doesn't let your mental machinery shut off at night. You'll lay there and start outlining summary arguments, and before you know it, it's sunrise again and there's a new potential client waiting in a holding cell who caught sight of one of your bus bench, billboard, or Internet ads and figures you are *just the guy* to get him out of this little old "ice-pick mass murder" rap he's stumbled into.

Most attorneys fit some part of what I've described. But there are enough of another kind of lawyer that I'm ready to let you in on some secrets in the hopes that you will learn to spot these schmucks. The type who pad their bills. Who don't communicate. Who couldn't care less what happens once you hit the courtroom, but will still bill you like clockwork before the deputies snap the cuffs on your found-guilty wrists. And then, when you get that bill and are simmering with rage that you owe money to such a waste of carbon, they'll follow up with a collections phone call because the lease payment on their two-year-old BMW is overdue.

Make no mistake: even a lawyer who is a shitty lawyer still passed the bar and knows how to turn his ugly, infuriating loopholes into sparkly, symmetrical little bows before Mr. Average Hockey Dad with a DUI can look up how to dispute bills or actions that shitty lawyer supposedly made while working his case. The lawyer that seemed to be falling asleep in front of the judge will snap right to attention if she thinks her payday might be slipping away.

Here are a few things to consider:

- **If you signed a letter of agreement to retain your attorney when you two began your relationship, you should know that letter doesn't have squat to do with the fairness of whatever fees he or she charges you.** Most states have some kind of code of conduct that attorneys are bound to follow, and that code will frequently contain language that essentially says attorneys aren't allowed to take any illegal, overly burdensome fees. An engagement letter might lay out details of billing, as well as how the case might be pursued, but if those details aren't reasonable, a court can step in and reduce or even nullify fees.

- **If you are in the middle of a case and Bam-Bam, Esquire, takes his club of a law degree and whacks you with a request for a bonus above any agreed-upon fees, get suspicious real quick.** Agreed-upon payments have to be honored, sure, but the bonus is usually up to you. I say "usually" because the complicated laws surrounding this sort of thing can be twisted in a lawyer's favor depending on the state you're in—but generally, you have to abide by what you signed, and not some later request made because Bam-Bam wasn't paying attention when you originally explained your situation, and underestimated the amount of work the case was going to entail.

- **Study your bills.** I don't care if you think your attorney is the baby Jesus himself doing a solid gold job of dancing into a courtroom victory: look hard at each element of the bill. If you see even one itsy-bitsy thing that makes you say, "huh?"—raise a concern. It's just like buying a car. Those sneaky salesmen are going to try to charge you "floor plan" and "vehicle preparation" fees to get your new wheels off the showroom linoleum, but if you resist, they'll take them off lickety-split. Vetting an attorney's billing is the best way to find some mutually agreeable solution to knock a few bucks off a daunting invoice. And maybe if you're the first to call bullshit on an item like "domestic pet hair depilatory," the attorney will see the jig is up and stop trying to be so clever.

- **Attorneys, no matter how well-equipped they are with legal knowledge, don't like going through fee disputes.** Even less than most clients do, is my guess. If a client is 150 percent certain they are willing to dispute the fee, know that it can be pretty embarrassing to an attorney to have to deal with it. The dispute makes them look bad to other attorneys. A strongly disputed fee might even segue into a malpractice claim—and believe me, lawyers unanimously don't want their or their firms' names anywhere near the word "malpractice." Just like you would be horrified to have "accused sex offender" come up when you Google your name, we don't want even a hint of ethical wrongdoing associated with our work. That is not to say a fee dispute will scare a lawyer into submission. If you default to petty intimidation, the system and one really pissed-off attorney will steamroll you. But! A carefully appraised and detailed argument is serious business to an attorney, and they'll want to resolve it the best way possible if they have a lick of sense. Which might lead to . . .

- **Arbitration.** Look, if the fees at issue are not six-figure income killers, if the issue just isn't that *big*, the state bar can sometimes assist with a good old arbitration. If a client volunteers to get involved with arbitration, the lawyer usually has little choice but to go along. Buyer beware—frequently, an arbitration is just about the fees and nothing but the fees. If a client suspects there is another brand of sketchiness afoot in their counselor's shadowy offices—like, perhaps the attorney was bribed to throw the case—arbitration efforts won't stray from the money lane.

Shenanigans

Knowing the qualities worth seeking in a truly good attorney is one thing, and understanding some of the bullshit you don't have to put up with is another. There are plenty of things that might tip you off that your potential legal apple has a wormy lawyer hidden in its core. Determining whether you're looking at a red flag is a subjective art, sure. One man's too-slick crook might be another's legal life partner. Just like when you're scrutinizing whether that check-engine light flashing on your dashboard means you should pull over instead of continuing to cruise down a snowy highway, you might have to go with your gut. And, for what it's worth: you should probably pull over and check that light out. Your car probably isn't just trying to say, "Hey, thinking of you, we should hang out more."

- **The office.** Look for whatever shivers your timbers. For example: is it well-lit, with an impressive modern design? Is it reasonably neat? Look, law firms are constantly crushed under endless blizzards of paper, so make your expectations reasonable. An antiseptic microbe-free decontamination room won't necessarily be the standard, but you can reasonably expect to see that a little TLC goes into the place's upkeep. This goes for the attorney, too. They don't need to be decked in the *GQ*-est suits and Rolexes, but they should take pride in dressing for success. However: attorneys come in all stripes, and there have been some real geniuses who were complete slobs, or walking fashion faux pas, or wore crazy duds as a middle finger to conformists—so keep in mind that there might be a pearl worth polishing in the center of that barnacled oyster of an office.

- **Shitty attitude.** This is stony ground, because when people walk into a law office, chances are good they're feeling justifiably sensitive. Now, a thoughtful attorney is fully aware of this, and learns how to ride the fine line between being an honest advocate and an empathetic ear. Most folks are able to recognize the qualities of a dud: laziness, condescension, general smart-assery, etc. Those traits are about as subtle as an elephant competing in the Feline Olympics. On the other hand, if you've got someone who can crack a joke, lighten your load with laughter for even a second— that's the self-rowing paddle that's going to steer your leaky canoe up and out of Shit Creek while you're lying fetal between the gunwales. Your situation is serious enough as it is without having to deal with some Legal Crypt Keeper, sitting behind their desk and chattering about all the legal doom you face.

- **The ability to communicate.** Both ways— responding and initiating. And I'm talking about an office working with some kind of calendar system that organizes this communication. Look, if you fire off ten e-mails and not even the attorney's assistant's intern's hamster can be bothered to send back a "*¿Qué?*" then there's a problem in the law practice of Highfees, Dud, and Doolittle. If phones ring and ring and don't even go to a generic after-hours answering service, you're right to wonder, "Hey, what's up with that?" That's probably a failing practice, my friend. It's a little legal *Hindenburg* and it's about to catch fire.
- **Unrealistic promises.** What is realistic, anyway? A perfectly decent attorney isn't always above eye-

SIDEBAR

I don't know if it's true that for every case there is a perfect attorney. But, I like to believe there's a little something to it. So: maybe don't go galloping off with the first attorney you meet. That'll go over as well as waking up with a Vegas hangover, a wedding ring, and an introduction to your new future ex-husband. Don't settle for less; make sure your boxes are checked, but don't be too damned quick to judge. A snap judgment to hire the lawyer with the biggest ad campaign, for instance, might deprive you of a chance to cut through all the justice system's bullshit with the sharpest tool in the shed. On the flip side: those hardworking men and women asking for your business on late-night TV could be the hungriest and most passionate lawyers in town. There's a big advantage in having a clever and think-outside-the-box legal mind on your side.

So: read a few pages of the book before you judge the smiling, shiny cover. White teeth and a bespoke pinstripe suit may paint an attractive picture, but that colorful sports jacket and unforgettable slogan you see every time you take the midtown bus to the liquor store may be exactly the razzmatazz you need.

balling a particularly tasty case in which it looks like all the pins are perfectly aligned to bowl a big-ass strike and saying, "We've got this, relax, game over." But most of us know better than to say that. Be suspicious of an attorney's confidence, even their competence, the moment they say, "Piece of cake, it's already won." There are too many unpredictable elements in even the most milquetoast of misdemeanors to make that guarantee.

Summation

It's pretty simple, really: pay your counselors for the services they've rendered. We have a right to earn a living, and we've put in the hard work and the study to be where we are. In fact, pay *all* the folks who are working for you. And give your mail carrier a holiday bonus, Scrooge McDuck. It's the least you can do after ordering that fifty-pound vat of lube for home delivery last April.

Having said that, don't let yourself be taken advantage of, either. Nobody should feel stuck in a situation where they're being gouged, or talked down to, or generally cheated. Hell, you hired a lawyer to get you out of a jam—it's downright twisted for that lawyer to try to make things worse for you.

This takes some common sense on the client's part, and a heaping scoop of intuition and attention to detail.

If anything, figuring out that you've got a crappy attorney might just come down to a gut check. I knew a lawyer who was having a conversation with a client about a court appearance on charges the client was stealing from his church donations every Sunday. The lawyer had new cards to give out, and opened his wallet. As he did that, he made a big show of turning the wallet and the few hundred-dollar bills inside away from his client's view.

The guy wasn't necessarily a bad lawyer, but that's kind of an asshole move, right? Sure enough, that client—even though he was facing a tough case that could have ended with jail time—opted for different counsel. You can be killer at your job, but sometimes just a brief slip into the confirmed douchebag slot will be enough to lose a little face, not to mention present and future work.

See, it's not all on you, the client. You're not a contestant on one of those "So You Think You're a Temptress" island brothel shows—or, if you are, you're the one in the sexy hula skirt handing out the lei to your lawyer of choice. In all my "do this, don't do that," maybe I haven't been clear enough about the fact that you are a hot commodity, you're the creamy bowl of tomato bisque that's going to feed one lucky hungry counselor. You deserve respect, not to mention the best defense that money can buy.

PART IV

Avoiding Temptation

The Straight but Not
Necessarily Narrow Life

I love my work. I enjoy gently guiding clients through the mean streets of the justice system, and I understand that sometimes even honor roll students end up in the back of a squad car, staring at their reflection in the window and asking themselves what the heck just happened.

Whatever it was that put you there—a drug deal, public urination, dognapping—you don't want to repeat the misadventure. Don't worry about keeping my practice in business, because there are many, many other things a canny entrepreneur like me can help you out with—all of them well within the boundaries of Farmer

Five-O's happy ranch of admissible activities. What I'm talking about now is more about taking off my lawyer hat (because we've already gotten you off the hook) and putting on my life coach cap. Here follows a few thoughts on how to keep your nose clean, as far as the authorities are concerned.

Make It Work for You

You're familiar with judo; it's that smooth-looking martial art deployed with pizzazz by most spies in old espionage flicks. It's no accident that judo translates to "gentle way"—it may look like make-believe when a tiny little gumshoe upends a beefy henchman, but it's all about gracefully turning the enemies' own weight and balance against them.

Stay with me, here. The trick to successfully flipping your career in crime into a more respectable aboveboard way of life is to take the very thing dragging you down and turn it to your advantage.

I'm going to give some examples of folks who were this kind of judo master (I don't know if any of them were actual judo masters). Then we'll talk about what you can do to figure out what your hidden talent might be. Maybe you're an innovator, a strategist, or mentorin-disguise. One man's spray-can-wielding hoodlum is another's undiscovered Keith Haring.

Frank

They made a movie about Frank Abagnale. Starring Tom Hanks and Leonardo DiCaprio, no less. Frank was a prodigy. He was gifted at being other guys. He started early, the Mozart of fraud and deception. Frank was fifteen when he figured out a way to chisel more than $3,000 from his own father. It was only up from there. Frank soon began to joyfully bounce forged checks. He set up a false bank deposit situation, ended up walking off with sacks of cash directly from the banks themselves.

A man of the many-colored cloth, Frank liked to try on different looks. He impersonated an airline pilot and flew something like a million miles for free. The guy masqueraded as a doctor for almost a year. He was a chameleon.

Frank Abagnale even posed as an attorney—up to the point of passing the bar exam. All by the time he was legally old enough to buy a case of beer at the corner store.

Overachiever, right? Frank was arrested in France when he was twenty-one. He continued to impress, and escaped from a federal prison (don't try this at home, kids)—but eventually he did do a little time. After he got out and cycled through some uninteresting, everyday gigs, Frank began selling his criminal banking expertise to the banks he might have been ripping off. He'd demonstrate the many ways con artists could cheat these financial institutions, so that they could learn to better protect their customers from people with Frank's skills. This turned into a legitimate business that he was still running well into his sixties.

Every con man survives on being able to weave an entertaining fib, so it's a little hard to tell how much of Frank's story is true, but even if only half of his exploits really went down the way he tells, the guy was some kind of larcenous savant.

Frank's famous today because he took that wily criminal expertise and turned it on its head. Not everyone has his brainiac attention to detail or his charm-their-pants-off smile, but any halfway decent criminal has a glitter of something in them that can be discovered, mined, and smelted in fine golden jewelry.

Georgia

The next time you're cruising down the highway, take a second glance at some of those beautiful blonde bombshells that you see plastered over billboards selling everything from sunglasses to buffalo wings, and think about Georgia Durante. In the 1970s, Georgia was a model in upstate New York, a "Kodak Girl"—the epitome of vintage urban glamour back when you still had to snap a flashcube to the top of your point-and-shoot if you wanted to take a picture in anything short of direct sunlight. While she was still a teenager, she fell in love and fell in with the mafia. One night, someone tossed her a set of keys, told her to get going, and soon the mob discovered that this girl could *drive*.

Knowing how to put the pedal to the metal is an ability that can be put to use if you're running with a bad crowd. Georgia found herself the go-to getaway driver for the mafia, and probably had some fun for a while, but then a mob war broke out, and she had to skip town. While trying to keep a low profile in sunny California, she found the perfect way to use her skills to keep her family afloat: stunt driving. As a stunt double, her face was always obscured, but she got to skid-and-spin her heart out. She took something that made her a successful criminal and reinvented herself—now she's happily enjoying her retirement as an author, speaking at prisons, and advocating for abused women. That's some beautiful judo magic, my friend.

Kevin

Once, Kevin Mitnick was the most wanted hacker in the world. His mug graced our TVs, courtesy of the great old series *Unsolved Mysteries*. Kevin hacked damned near everyone, his shenanigans detailed by news reports from here to Timbuktu. It started with a few free bus rides when he was a kid, then turned into something much, much greater. His crime streak began in the abacus-laden days of 1970s, so he seemed like some sort of mystical Norse god of binary runes.

Finally, Kevin's punch card ran out, and he was convicted for his cyber crimes. He served a year in prison, but once he was on the outside, he went back to his mischievous ways. Soon, his computer chicanery was discovered, and he became a fugitive. Kevin dodged Uncle Sam's hammer for a full two years while o'er the cyber fields he went, hacking all the way. The feds tracked him down, and he was put away for five more years. Take note, ladies and gentlemen—if they can catch Osama bin Laden in the rolling hills of Abbottabad, they can certainly find you sipping a mai tai in the lonely tiki lounge next door to the southernmost Greyhound station in the Florida Keys.

When he was released, Kevin was forbidden from using anything wired except a telephone—that's how much he'd spooked Big Brother. There were widespread urban legends about what the guy could do armed with only his wits and a networked Commodore 64.

Kevin appealed the computer restrictions, and they were lifted. He made good on his promise to make good—he took what he knew about computer security and started his own consulting company specializing in analyzing big systems owned by major businesses all over the country. Nowadays he shows up on the news occasionally, but not for any current misdeeds. He discusses cyber crime if some crazed hackers take over a bank, lift unassuming shoppers' credit card numbers, or dump their targets' private information on the Web for all the world to see.

All this to say: sometimes "going straight" (living a life free of any questionable activities that might necessitate the services of fine counselors like yours truly) doesn't require as many adjustments as you might think.

Sure, that's qualified—crimes that have to do with abusing substances, for example, kind of carry an inherent demand the persons convicted do something about their unpleasant dependencies. But! There are criminal pursuits that require skills you can modify to use to your, and society's, advantage.

Imagine a woman arrested for cheating a casino. She had some kind of system—collusion, card marking, maybe even counting—that allowed her to rack up a rainbow of ill-gotten chips. No matter how she did it, she found a way to evade the casino's security protocols much longer than previous card sharks, so catching her was just pure dumb luck.

Casino owners will be interested in how this woman pulled it off. Sure, they could probably figure it out by combing through whatever investigative documents are created by the detectives on the case, or they can simply cut through the pantomime and approach the hustler directly to say, "Hey, tell us what you did here." I'm not saying you should break the magician's code, Valentino, but maybe if the opportunity presents itself, it's time to lay a few of your cards on the table.

Now let me tell you about a former client of mine, Slim Jim. He was a pro with a crowbar, boosting cars left and right for midnight joyrides. He'd fence the stereos, nab the plates, then ditch the wheels in the parking lot of the closest Blake's Lotaburger. Slim was in no position to take I-40 straight to Hollywood and make it big like Georgie, but you know what he did to turn his temptation into an honest trade? He became a taxi driver. Now he gets to pick things up and put them right back down someplace else all day long, and if someone's running late for a flight to their daughter's wedding, well, they certainly don't mind if he puts a little extra weight on the accelerator pedal.

So, what's tempting to you? Easy money? That tempts everyone, get in line! Washing your problems away with a sweet swig of Kentucky bourbon? Not having to worry about taxes and paperwork and qualifying for a mortgage? Congratulations, then: you're a human with a heartbeat and mortal temptations.

Sometimes that's all "criminal activity" really is—someone giving in to the most basic human hungers. That doesn't excuse breaking the law, but it does make a difference on the inside. Screwing up can be a vicious cycle of giving in to your most base desires, realizing what you've done, hating yourself for it—then feeling gutted by the hate and screwing up again. And like these folks I just told you about, you, too, can (and should!) identify your skills and use them to your advantage.

Maybe you've been convicted, for example, of some kind of con game that involves being really good at persuasion. That's a very special skill, one that works outside of crime, sometimes brilliantly. You can smoothly talk someone out of their hard-earned money doing a kind of bait and switch? I'd bet you'd kick ass at selling cars. Or selling anything.

Summation

It all comes down to one phrase: "Don't give up." Facing a legal snafu can do a real number on you, and make you feel like waving the white flag. Cops and prosecutors trying to put you away; your reputation and your livelihood on the line—this is how spirits get broken and families fall apart. But: hang in there, baby!

When the going gets rough, that's when whatever "special skills" you've used to get you where you are might work in your favor and help you survive. Even if you receive a not-guilty verdict, the road ahead can look like it's got more shitty hairpin turns than you'd find twisted up in your small intestine.

Sometimes, an acquittal can be even better for your fate than not getting in trouble in the first place. What the hell were you up to when the accusation came your way, anyway? Even if you were totally on the up and up, and the allegations of criminal behavior were completely unwarranted, what you face now is—*voilà!*—a chance to change, be a better you, all that jazz. And the slow path to self-improvement is a lot more pleasant than the fast track to lockup.

You Must Change Your Life

I've talked about planning—about putting contingencies in place. This is all between your attorney and you, discussed in-office or in whispers in court when you can get away with it.

These conversations are all "before." It's only natural to wonder about the "after." When you're in the middle of a trial, it's like you're clinging to flotsam and ice floes right off the sinking *Titanic*. You're happy to be alive and above water, but somewhere in the back of your soggy cerebellum you've got to be thinking, "The ship's long gone . . . what's the plan now?" Everything that follows, whether you win or lose your case, is the "after" and it needs some love, too. How we manage the "after" has a heck of a lot to do with whether a client ends up a repeat customer or not. Hey, I want to see you again, of course! But first you can do a little solo legwork to restore yourself once the ordeal of court is over.

And if you lose your case, that doesn't mean you're done. We've talked about how to make the best of your potential time behind bars, but most clients—even the toughest meatheads in the joint—still have something on the outside that keeps their hearts ticking and encourages them to continue drawing big, fat Xs on the calendar days to mark their time.

If even Big Bubba is angling at how to get his affairs in order on the outside, I know for sure that you will be, too.

Unfortunately, just having a sharp new suit or Liberace feather boa or whatever your flavor laid out all nice and ironed when you strip off that prison jumpsuit probably isn't going to be the only big fix you need to put your life back on track again. We know there's much more to it than that, but I can use that as a symbol.

Whatever position you're in, once it's all over—the trial itself, the sentence after the trial—it's *over* and that's awesome. We start in the black again, right?

When you get out, your perspective is going to be different. It's like what people say about near-death experiences—you come out to see the grass grows greener, the cinnamon buns smell sweeter, the chili tastes spicier, and the ocean breeze feels just a bit breezier.

If you've been in lockup it might be easy—*really* easy—to walk out into the world with a grade-A chip on your shoulder. Many people do. They end up back in my office, too, because that anger is jet fuel for a big term: "recidivism." It sounds like something that involves a high fever and brings out boils on your skin, but it's just a fancy word for "relapse."

Energy can't be created or destroyed; it's science! For these aforementioned ladies and gents all that anger they're carrying needs someplace to go, so they might find themselves taking it out on someone. That can happen even if the case is won, since trials are so stressful.

However you're feeling, a new set of clothes might be a good first move toward your fresh-smelling new lease on life. Some other steps to consider taking:

- **Don't do the same shit you used to do.** Sounds like a lead-pipe cinch, but did you ever go sledding as a kid? Find a hill covered in fresh, fluffy snow, sit yourself down on a trashcan lid, and—*wheee!*—down the slope you go. First time's a little slow, there's no natural path so you're carving it yourself—but the more times you ride down, a clear route starts to form and it becomes really, really hard to break out of that groove. The bad business you're associated with? That's the groove. I've mentioned it before, talking about running with old friends who might only get you in trouble again. Let's broaden that horizon. Don't even take the same routes you used to walk through the neighborhood to get to the corner store. Nobody wants to remain as unsettled as they feel after a trial—or worse, an incarceration (I get indigestion just thinking about it)—but it might be a chance to instate some good new habits.

- **Get a job.** It can be tough for those who are having a lover's quarrel with the law to find work, even if they were on trial but never convicted, because that alone gives you an arrest record. Like if a guy or gal is tried for taking pervy Polaroids at the state fair—even if they're found not guilty, you're not gonna sign up for their bargain glamour photo shoot next summer. The good news is that there are services in place in a lot of cities that are geared toward helping folks with legal issues find jobs. They find employers who believe in giving people second chances. That's pretty great. But, to be clear, if you're working with a program like this, you've got to manage your expectations. Regardless of the job you were doing before your scuffle with the law, your entrée back into the workforce may be severely limited. I don't care what a whiz he is with a calculator,

SIDEBAR

We've been talking a lot about strategy. Strategy has nothing to do with some kind of touchy-feely, flowing linen and starshine kind of "Fix my life" bull hockey. It's about an honest client and a no-nonsense lawyer who recognize that people are gonna try to be who they are and that it may be necessary to manage how others see that.

Think about this statement: "The clothes make the con." The con as in "confidence." As in conviction. That new dress? That new suit? An Italian wool tool. It says you're ready for a new start, and *look like* a different person. Just because you're putting on a costume doesn't mean you've become the role. Leave that to Streep and Pacino.

nobody's asking for Bernie Madoff to manage their finances anymore. So, cool it with the hubris—the best job available may not be a golden ticket to a new life ripe with velvet carpets and gold-plated toilet seats, but it may still be the yellow brick road that leads you back to happiness and stability.

- **Take it down a notch.** Are you animated? Not like: are you a cartoon, Scratch Cat—but, do you have a big mouth? Vibrant personality? A memorable disposition that sometimes rubs folks quietly reading on the subway the wrong way? If you're trying to recoup your life, it may be time to back-pedal a little. Don't worry, no one is trying put your light under a bushel! I'd never try to change who you are. But! Being Mr. Low Profile might be a wise strategy to consider as a viable means of staying off the radar of Eliot Ness and his ragtime band.

Back to those positive steps:

- **Make yourself a better you (or at least a better image of you).** Consider joining a club. Maybe take a yoga class? If you were raised with a perfect Sunday School attendance record and stopping by a service or two doesn't make you grind your teeth to nubs, maybe even brings you inner peace or some quiet time—heck, go back! You could just zone out and work on your cryptograms while you're there, but when you're trying to present the latest, greatest you to the judge presiding over your probation? Church is awesome. Sing along with the hymns, join the bell choir, carry the heaviest boxes when it's time to host the town book sale. Work on your posture! That sort of thing looks great when you're checking in with your parole officer.

- **Mix and mingle.** When it comes to dating, don't let your criminal record stand in your way any more than you would your high school report card. This advice is obviously more for the unmarried client. If you're married and you want to start dating again, that's a fun new adventure or a hullabaloo that could end with you wading in a hefty new set of bills and a few more courtroom appearances. But for you singles out there, nothing looks better to ensure your continued conditional release than some kind of steady relationship. That's pretty much synonymous with stability. So: try it. If you're shy, start online. Whatever your preference or creed or ethnicity or farming experience, there's a dating site for you. There are a heck of a lot of fish in that (albeit murky) ocean. If you're an in-person kinda person, see if there are any babes at that library or church where you sit and do Sudoku, whatever— just keep in mind that the more steady things you have going on in life, the better it will start to feel and the better it will look to those who are paying more attention than you'd probably like them to.

Summation

The clothes you choose are like the strong whiff of per-
fume that's going to leave an impression after you walk
out of a room. But, outfits are just one aspect of your
metamorphosis. If your trial resulted in jail time, there
are ways to start working toward that transformation
before you put on your shades and walk out squinting at
the sunshine of freedom. One thing incarceration does
provide is time. It's yours for the taking. To work on
that novel, to learn a new language. I know of men and
women behind bars who slimmed from flabby to taut in
time to take on the world. There are others who come
out basically bar exam ready, because hey, if there's a law
library in there, why not get into it and start figuring out
what all those official-looking people were mumbling
about during the trial?

Better yourself . . . or at least fake it till you make
it. On some level, everything we're out here doing is a
con. The best ones don't really harm anyone. I'm not
trying to take you shopping—I'm trying to help you
understand how to survive in a system that's sometimes set up to work against you. A new suit is just the
first step.

A New You!

Here's something to ponder: is it really identity theft if they're dead?

As an officer of the court, I can't give you any tips or tricks that illuminate the road to extralegal behavior. That is against everything I know about the New Mexico State Bar! But—let's say you were in a doozy of a lose-lose situation. Your attorney knows it. You know it. (Stipulation before we wade into this swamp—I'm assuming for argument's sake that this is a situation where you've made bail and can roam the countryside as you await trial.)

Maybe talking renewal, a chance to build things back up, all that is just smoke to you. It will feel like measles soaked in consumption dipped in typhoid to do time. It might even lead to literal death. It's not unheard of, for example, for informants—whistle-blowers—to end up behind bars alongside some of the people they blew whistles about. That situation rarely ends in butterflies and rainbows.

So: how new a new you are we talking about? Let me back up. What constitutes identity theft, after all?

Stealing a living person's identity is a pretty nasty patch of brambles. It's this big wholesale fraud, and it can get you put away until your grandkids' grandkids' cows come home.

The Internet has also made it pretty damned common, because so much of our lives are online. All the ones and zeroes that make you the special you that you are. Here's how the identity theft you hear about every day might go down:

Vlad, a hacker in Ukraine, calls up the systems administrator for the computer network at your job, let's say. Vlad figures out a way to con a master key kind of password out of the gal. Vlad weasels into your hosted server honeypot and starts downloading boatloads of information. He gets a lot of names, addresses, social security numbers—for all you know there's even a scan of your birth certificate and social security card. Then, Vlad sells that data mine on some Internet black market.

Meanwhile, someone in Arizona has crappy credit and wants to shop online at leisure. They buy your info from Vlad and set up all sorts of dummy accounts they can use to charge bills that will never actually get paid. Perhaps your bank info is involved, and then the whimsical cyber shopper will hole up in Tucson and start draining your funds. A drib at first, then a drab, then a deluge that even the Hoover Dam couldn't control.

That's the quick-and-dirty on one kind of identity

theft. It happens every day, and trying to fight it is like running into a hurricane with your fists and an umbrella. It might end up ruining your credit or leaving you broke, if you find yourself the victim and not the perpetrator. I think you get the picture.

But let's go back to the question of a new you. There's another kind of identity theft with a creepy name: ghosting. This is when someone steals the identity of a dead fella, maybe even acts as that person. It relies on targeting someone who others barely know is deceased. That can be especially unsettling if the thief did the killing, but let's keep a happy thought and assume that the hypothetical ghost is of the friendly Casper variety, and just happened to notice that a miserly hermit with no relatives passed away before their time.

Ghosting isn't easy. It's probably harder to pull off now than it once was, what with the Internet around to keep a near-infinite record of each person's existence, or in this case, former existence. One driver's license search by a cop in Nebraska might trigger red flags on a computer in California. And ghosting isn't about fast heaps of cash, either. It's a way to become a new person. To go off your old grid and onto a completely new one. I wouldn't call it a fresh start, but people are all about recycling these days.

Don't get me wrong. I'll emphasize it: no way I'm

telling anyone how to do this. We're just spitballing. An off-the-record chat dealing strictly in hypotheticals.

A person with the goal of ghosting another identity to, say, get out of being murdered—or at least arrested— would need to study up and get organized. They'd have to become a real straight-A student of obituaries or brush up on their smooth-talking to get in cozy with the funeral director's daughter. They'd be looking for some key things: hometown, date of birth, parents' full names, employment history, job history. Then they might call up the vital records office and order the death certificate bearing the dearly departed's social security. Thus begins the ghosting.

This actually worked like gangbusters twenty to thirty years ago. There's no telling how many ghosts have spent their golden years in someone else's golden years, maybe only being outed at death—if then.

Today, though? Gets harder with every smartphone update, but still not impossible for a person with the right chutzpah! Thieves are still using it to shotgun fake tax returns to the IRS using the social security numbers of the recently deceased, netting a few million a year.

Why does it work at all in a world where the World Wide Web just keeps spinning thick digital threads connecting everything and everyone? These wily ghosts seize their tiny windows of opportunity like Indiana

Jones snatching his sable fedora seconds before the wall caves in. Bereaved families often have more pressing matters than letting the Social Security Administration know that their loved one is gone. And often, no one even thinks to let credit agencies know that the name attached to that social has left the building and it's probably a misstep to extend them a new line of credit. And the credit agencies don't exactly allot much proactive manpower to vetting bad ideas.

But, yes: it *is* still identity theft if the person is dead. I'm definitely not advising you to ever consider such a thing. It's a fun campfire story, though, right?

The idea of suddenly leaving your cares behind and beginning a different life is appealing. Sometimes people just want to get the hell away and reboot. Start anew, fresh as a daisy. Disappear. If that's what you're looking for, I can't say I advise it, but . . . I may know a guy that can help you out.

Final Summation

Well, buddy, we've covered the bases, the outfield, the bleachers, the concourse, and the hot dog stand.

It's no legal textbook, because only law professors with tenure and sabbaticals have time to hunch over their keyboards for that long, and bless them and the fast-typing grad students they're putting through the wringer.

We had to make this glance at the criminal justice system speedy because that's all most people have time for these days. If that's you, I hope I helped a smidge. If you have a bit more time, grab hold of any legal nuggets that have lodged themselves in your brain and pop them into your favorite search engine, because plenty of attorneys are out there slinging free advice for the taking.

To recap a little: it's your right as a citizen of this great democracy to stand in the dock and argue on your own behalf. But don't go for that brass ring without understanding what you're getting into, and Jesus, Mary, Joseph, Stills, and Nash—friend, please understand how much a professional lawyer can do in your corner. We made it our job to learn how to argue for you. Just remember Ted Bundy—good enough in court to earn a compliment from the judge, but old Ted still ended up fricasseed by Old Sparky.

Seriously, if you are that compelled to represent yourself, go for it. Buckle down and be certain that—worst-case scenario—you are going to be the most shockingly good pro se defender to ever lose a case in that judge's court.

We talked about a few of the many instances when

you might really need an attorney. It's a hard old world, full of opportunities to just screw it all up, over and over again. You learn the hard way that no one warns you beforehand, "Oh, shit, you will end up needing a lawyer if you do that."

I could bottom-line all those moments just by saying, "Be careful out there." This isn't *Hill Street Blues*, though, and most people are a little more careful than not. Life just has a messed-up way of surprising us sometimes.

While we've been under the hood tinkering with everything from bench warrants to homicide, I've tried to keep one simple theme thumping along, like the hook of a pop song from the eighties. Preparing for legal ordeals means just that: preparing. It's my business and my pleasure to talk strategy, every day. A typical suburban dad in his eco-conscious SUV may come close to this mind-set the day of his fantasy football draft, sure, but past that it won't occur to him.

And when it comes to avoiding temptation? People come into a law office, they sit down to discuss their case, and we lawyers start to see the bumpy, potholed, and winding roads that led them to us. That's why folks need new beginnings.

New beginnings are marvelous creatures. Even better than a visit from the Tooth Fairy or Easter Bunny or whatever mythical creature validated your childhood. No one should take advantage of anyone else to get a fresh start, though. And once you put the right foot forward, you've got the chance to look back on what you did before and see where you could've sat out an inning and maybe not broken your pelvis stealing third base.

Wherever you are, whatever the situation—when you have to make the acquaintance of one of the brave and hardworking members of your local law enforcement community, the thing you need to remember before the cogs of justice start grinding away is this: seal your lips and lawyer up.

In the meantime, carpe diem with the cuffs off while I go tango with Lady Justice.